Collins

Cambridge Lower Secondary

English
as a Second
Language

Anna Osborn

Series Editor: Nick Coates

STAGE 8: WORKBOOK

William Collins' dream of knowledge for all began with the publication of his first book in 1819.

A self-educated mill worker, he not only enriched millions of lives, but also founded a flourishing publishing house. Today, staying true to this spirit, Collins books are packed with inspiration, innovation and practical expertise. They place you at the centre of a world of possibility and give you exactly what you need to explore it.

Collins. Freedom to teach.

Published by Collins
An imprint of HarperCollins*Publishers*
The News Building
1 London Bridge Street
London
SE1 9GF

Browse the complete Collins catalogue at
www.collins.co.uk

ISBN 978-0-00-821546-0

British Library Cataloguing in Publication Data

A catalogue record for this publication is available from the British Library.

Author: Anna Osborn
Development editor: Alison Ramage
Series Editor: Nick Coates
Commissioning editor: Lucy Cooper
In-house editor: Lara McMurray
Project Manager: Anna Stevenson
Copyeditor: Sarah Dev-Sherman
Answer checker: Sonya Newland
Proofreader: Karen Williams
Cover designer: Kevin Robbins
Cover illustrator: Maria Herbert-Liew
Typesetter: Jouve India Private Ltd
Illustrator: QBS Learning
Production controller: Rachel Weaver

Printed and bound by Martins the Printers

Acknowledgements

The publishers gratefully acknowledge the permission granted to reproduce the copyright material in this book. Every effort has been made to trace copyright holders and to obtain their permission for the use of copyright material. The publishers will gladly receive any information enabling them to rectify any error or omission at the first opportunity.

Key: t = top, b = bottom, l = left, r = right, c = centre

p5 Fer Gregory/Shutterstock, p10 Monkey Business Images/Shutterstock, p12 sondem/Shutterstock, p13 Phase4Studios/Shutterstock, p16 wavebreakmedia/Shutterstock, p17l lzf/Shutterstock, p17r Billion Photos/Shutterstock, p18 fotoinfot/Shutterstock, p20 wavebreakmedia/Shutterstock, p23 Oleg Krugliak/Shutterstock, p26 Mike Focus/Shutterstock, p30 Anton Rogozin/Shutterstock, p32tl Ammit Jack/Shutterstock, p32tc AlexZaitsev/Shutterstock, p32tr djgis/Shutterstock, p32bl blvdone/Shutterstock, p32bc Tisha 85/Shutterstock, p32br Nonchanon/Shutterstock, p32b iFerol/Shutterstock, p33 Wim Hoek/Shutterstock, p37 Konstanttin/Shutterstock, p42 Iakov Filimonov/Shutterstock, p46 DVARG/Shutterstock, p48 Irina Nartova/Shutterstock, p53 Wang An Qi/Shutterstock, p58tl wavebreakmedia/Shutterstock, p58tc Toa55/Shutterstock, p58tr Likoper/Shutterstock, p58bl Rawpixel.com/Shutterstock, p58bc Cameron Whitman/Shutterstock, p58br leungchopan/Shutterstock, p69 Dean Drobot/Shutterstock, p80 Peeradach R/Shutterstock

Contents

Film and drama

Vocabulary: types of film

SB p.8

Complete the crossword.

Across
1 a serious film
3 a film with singing
5 a film about real life
6 a film set in the future (2 words)

Down
2 a cartoon (2 words)
4 a funny film

Reading: comprehension

SB p.9

Answer the questions.

1 Which film is a sequel? _____

2 Who wrote *Tom's Dream*? _____

3 What year is *Don't Look Back* set in? _____

4 Where does the main character in *Mouse on Goal* live? _____

5 Who directed *Sweet Fun*? _____

6 When is *Tom's Dream* set? _____

Reading: thinking about the text

SB p.9

Reading tip

Looking at the adjectives that writers use is a good way of understanding their opinions. They will use positive adjectives to describe things they like and negative adjectives to describe things that they don't like.

1 **Answer the questions.**

   1 Which of the films does the writer of the reviews like?

   _____

2 What adjectives do they use that make you understand this?

_____

3 Which of the films does the writer _not_ like?

_____

4 What adjectives do they use that make you understand this?

_____

2 **What's your opinion of the films in these reviews? Complete the sentences.**

1 I'd like to watch _____ (name of film) because _____.

2 I wouldn't like to watch _____ (name of film) because _____.

Vocabulary: talking about films

SB p.10

1 **Complete the sentences with the people who make films.**

| actor   main character   director   ~~writer~~ |

1 I'm the ¹ <u>writer</u> of the film – the script is all my work.

2 I was in charge of how the film was made – I'm the ² _____.

3 I'm a professional ³ _____ – I played the ⁴ _____ in this film.

2 **Write the nouns used to talk about films next to the correct definitions.**

| setting   ~~sequel~~   plot   special effects   acting   script |

1 <u>sequel</u>: a film that follows on from an earlier film.
2 _____: where a film takes place.
3 _____: the written words the actors speak.
4 _____: the story of a film.
5 _____: special techniques used to make unusual scenes in films.
6 _____: the way the actors perform in a film.

3 **Write the adjectives in the correct column of the table.**

| ~~realistic~~   unoriginal   disappointing   extraordinary   unrealistic   original |

Adjectives to say a film is good	Adjectives to say a film is bad
realistic	_____
_____	_____
_____	_____

Use of English: verbs + –ing forms

SB p.10

1 **Look and match.**

1 suggest	**a** to like doing something
2 avoid	**b** to tell someone what you think they should do
3 enjoy	**c** to say that you are happy with all the choices
4 not mind	**d** to do something regularly so you get better at it
5 practise	**e** to choose not to do something

2 **Write sentences.**

1 We / not mind / stay / here / for now.
We do not mind staying here for now.

2 She / avoid / play / basketball / yesterday.

_____

3 They / practise / score goals / every day.

_____

4 We / enjoy / eat / in restaurants.

_____

5 He / suggest / go / to the cinema.

_____

3 **Read and complete the sentences.**

1 *"Let's go to the cafe."*
Simon suggested _____

2 *"I never watch animated films."*
Lucy avoids _____

3 *"I'm happy to watch a drama and I'm happy to watch a comedy."*
Lauren doesn't mind _____

Speaking: making plans

SB p.12

Choose the best sentences on page 8 to complete the conversation.

Sarah: Let's get together next week.

Maria: ¹ _____ C _____

Sarah: Sorry, I have plans on Tuesday.

Maria: ² _____

Sarah: I don't have anything planned for Wednesday.

Maria: ³ _____

Sarah: That would be fun.

Maria: ⁴ _____

Sarah: I don't really like documentaries.

Maria: ⁵ _____

Sarah: Sounds good. I'll call you later and we can make a plan.

A What are you doing on Wednesday?

B Me too. I like films.

C Good idea! Are you busy on Tuesday?

D I prefer watching comedies to sci-fi.

E Oh, OK, how about watching a comedy?

F Shall we go to the cinema?

G Let's watch that new documentary.

Use of English: revision of future forms

SB p.13

1 Read and circle the correct option.

Dear Grandma,

I'm writing to tell you all my exciting plans. Tomorrow, I ¹_____ to the cinema with Lucy to watch a science-fiction film. It's all about what life ²_____ like in the future. I think it ³_____ brilliant! The film ⁴_____ at 5p.m. and then after the film we ⁵_____ dinner with her parents in a restaurant in town.

I hope you have a good time on holiday next week. ⁶_____ me some photographs? I ⁷_____ to show Mum this time!

⁸_____ on Sunday to say goodbye? Let me know what time is good for you.

Love,
Sarah

1 a will go	**b** go	**c** 'm going to go	**d** 's going to go
2 a is	**b** be	**c** will be	**d** is being
3 a is	**b** will be	**c** be	**d** won't be
4 a is beginning	**b** begins	**c** are going to begin	**d** begin
5 a 'm having	**b** 's having	**c** 're having	**d** will having
6 a You send	**b** Will you send	**c** Are you sending	**d** Do you send
7 a won't forget	**b** am not forgetting	**c** don't forget	**d** forget
8 a I call you	**b** Am I going to call you	**c** Shall I call you	**d** Am I calling you

Focus on Drama

SB p.14

1 Number the stages of the scene in the correct order.

☐ Colin sees the lines on the wall.

☐ Pixie finds Richard's diary.

☐ 1 The children arrive at the house.

☐ They talk about the paintings.

☐ They find the door and go through it.

☐ Lightning lights up the door on the wall.

2 **Read and match.**

1 List of characters
2 Act (n)
3 Scene
4 Stage instructions

a one of the smaller parts a play is divided into
b information for the actors about how to act the play
c this tells you about who is in the play and what they are like
d one of the main parts a play is divided into

3 **Write the words next to the correct definitions.**

| brave | ~~frightened~~ | silly | joking | wonder | shy | nervous | confident |

1 <u>frightened:</u>   afraid
2 _____ :   willing to do things that are dangerous without showing fear
3 _____ :   a feeling of great surprise or admiration
4 _____ :   worried about talking to people you don't know well
5 _____ :   worried about something
6 _____ :   feeling sure of your abilities and ideas
7 _____ :   something said in a way to make you laugh
8 _____ :   not behaving in a sensible way

Check your progress

1 What can you do now?

I can …

read and write film reviews ☐

use verbs + –ing forms ☐

understand and use phrases for making plans ☐

use a mixture of future forms ☐

act out and write a scene from a play ☐

My learning

What did you learn in this unit?

2 Answer the questions about this unit.

1 What have you enjoyed most?

_____

2 Is there anything you have found difficult?

_____

3 What would you like to learn more about?

_____

2   Being a good sport

Reading: understanding the text

SB p.19

1   Look again at the text. Where do you think you are most likely to see a questionnaire like this?

   a in a leaflet giving information about a sports club

   b in a sports magazine

   c in a book about a famous person who plays sports

2   Read and match the questions from the Student's Book.

   1 Question 1 is about

   2 Questions 2 and 3 are about

   3 Question 4 is about

   a what really matters in sport.

   b respecting adults who are in charge of the game.

   c behaving well whether you win or lose.

3   Look at the answers that you gave in Activity 2 of the Student's Book and answer these questions.

   1 Why do the **a** answers make you think that this person isn't a good sport?

   _____

   2 Why do the **b** answers make you think that this person is trying to be a good sport?

   _____

   3 Why do the **c** answers make you think this person is a good sport?

   _____

Reading: comprehension

SB p.19

Answer the questions.

1 Why should we respect the referee and the coach?

_____

2 Why do you think we should behave well whether we win or lose?

_____

3 What do you think is the most important thing about playing sport and why?

_____

Vocabulary: sporting verbs

Match the words with their meanings.

| congratulate | respect | ~~celebrate~~ | sulk | cheat | argue |

1 mark a happy event _celebrate_

2 do something that is not honest because you want to get something _____

3 have a good opinion of someone _____

4 be silent for a while because you're angry about something _____

5 express pleasure that something good has happened to someone _____

6 disagree with someone about something _____

Use of English: comparing things

1 Read and tick the correct sentence.

1 Henri finishes the walk in 32 minutes. Karl finishes the walk in 1 hour 14 minutes.
  a Henri walks much faster than Karl. ☐
  b Henri walks just as fast as Karl. ☐

2 Jack is 1 m 26 cm. Laurence is 1 m 25 cm
  a Laurence is much shorter than Jack. ☐
  b Laurence is slightly shorter than Jack. ☐

3 A cheetah can run 120 km/hour. A tiger can run 65 km/hour.
  a A tiger can't run as fast as a cheetah. ☐
  b A tiger can run much faster than a cheetah. ☐

4 Simon is $13\frac{1}{2}$ years old. Claudia is $13\frac{1}{2}$ years old.
  a Claudia isn't as old as Simon. ☐
  b Claudia is just as old as Simon. ☐

2 Complete the second sentence in each pair to mean the same as the first. Use the words _just as_, _slightly_, _much_ and _as_.

1 Mary is 1 m 3 cm and Yiangos is 1 m 76 cm.
Yiangos is _much taller than_ Mary.

2 Foti is 25 and Ahmed is 26.
Ahmed is _____ Foti.

3 Pete ran 14 km/hour and Chris ran 14 km/hour.
Pete ran _____ Chris.

4 Calan types 30 words a minute and Luca types 10 words a minute.
Luca doesn't _____ Calan.

Vocabulary: sporting competitions

Review the meanings of the italic words in the questions. Use them in your answers.

1 What's your greatest sporting *achievement*?

_____

2 Have you ever won a *medal*? What colour and for what sport?

_____

_____

3 Who is your favourite *professional athlete* and why?

_____

_____

4 Which sports team do you *admire* most and why?

_____

5 Have you ever done a *triathlon*? Would you like to? Why?/Why not?

_____

Vocabulary: sporting adjectives

1 Write in the missing letters to make five sporting adjectives.

   1 c _ mp _ titi _ e: wanting to be more successful than other people

   2 s _ ro _ g: healthy, with good muscles

   3 un _ it: not healthy or strong

   4 h _ rd-w _ rkin _ : doing something seriously with a lot of effort

   5 l _ z _ : not wanting to work

2 Complete the sentences with adjectives from Activity 1 and explain your choices.

   1 I would describe myself as _____ because _____.

   2 I wouldn't describe myself as _____ because _____.

1 **Choose the correct option.**

I ¹*have been* a professional athlete for six years. My greatest sporting achievement ² _____ when I won a gold medal in the triathlon at the Olympics. I thought the swimming was the hardest part of the race. While I ³ _____ , my leg suddenly ⁴ _____ to hurt.

I thought the race was over for me, but I ⁵ _____ going.

When I crossed the finished line, I realised that I ⁶ _____ first!

1 a was	b ~~have been~~	c was being	d had been
2 a was	b have been	c was being	d had been
3 a swam	b have swum	c was swimming	d had swum
4 a started	b has started	c was starting	d had started
5 a kept	b have kept	c was keeping	d had kept
6 a came	b have come	c was coming	d had come

2 **Write the verbs in the correct past tense.**

1 By the time I got to the stadium, the race _____ (finish).

2 This athlete _____ (win) a lot of medals so far this year.

3 When I was a little boy, I _____ (play) football every day after school before I hurt my knee.

4 He _____ (ride) his bicycle when he saw me.

5 My team and I _____ (celebrate) our win last week.

6 The player _____ (argue) with the referee when I arrived.

1 Find six reflexive pronouns and use them to complete the sentences below.

h	z	i	m	y	s	e	l	f	t
u	q	g	x	y	x	p	a	w	x
o	u	r	s	e	l	v	e	s	c
f	o	n	m	b	s	q	n	u	k
x	s	x	l	i	t	s	e	l	f
t	h	e	m	s	e	l	v	e	s
z	p	v	j	j	x	u	e	a	s
m	y	p	h	e	r	s	e	l	f
c	c	w	n	p	x	s	g	j	b
h	i	m	s	e	l	f	b	l	i

1 We helped _____ to some food.

2 He fell over, but he didn't hurt _____.

3 She made _____ a sandwich.

4 The cat washed _____ after its meal.

5 I saw _____ in the shop window.

6 They looked after _____ while their parents were out.

2 Write two sentences including the word *myself.*

_____

_____

Check your progress

1 What can you do now?

I can …

complete and think about a questionnaire about being a good sport ☐

use a mixture of past tenses ☐

compare things and use reflexive pronouns ☐

talk and write a fact file about an athlete I admire ☐

understand a text about where sports were first played ☐

carry out a sports survey ☐

My learning
What did you learn in this unit?

2 Answer the questions about this unit.

1 What have you enjoyed most?

_____

2 Is there anything you have found difficult?

_____

3 What would you like to learn more about?

_____

Reading: comprehension
SB p.30

1 Read the article again. Read the sentences and write *true* or *false*. Correct any sentences that are false.

1 Some children can't go to school because they live too far away from their nearest school. _____

2 Some children in Bangladesh go to school on boats. _____

3 There is no school equipment on the school boats in Bangladesh. _____

4 Some children in Bangladesh go to school in Solar-Powered Internet Schools. _____

5 The children who talk about their travelling schools like them. _____

2 Complete the sentences.

The schools in the article are:

1 different to my school because _____.

2 similar to my school because _____.

Reading: scanning for specific information
SB p.30

Scan the text and answer these questions in two minutes. Time yourself!

1 What's the name of the student from South Africa? _____Lefa_____

2 Is the Solar-Powered Internet School made of metal or wood? _____

3 Where does Kakoli come from? _____

4 Where did the first Solar-Powered Internet School open? _____

5 What does Kakoli want to be when she grows up? _____

Vocabulary
SB p.30

1 Complete the dictionary entries with the words from the box.

| tablet | notebook | printer | whiteboard |

1 _____ (noun)
a machine that prints

2 _____ (noun)
where a teacher shows information in a classroom

3 _____ (noun)
a a small, thin computer
b a book of blank pages to write notes on

4 _____ (noun)
a a small, thin computer with a touchscreen
b a medicine that you eat

2 **Complete the text.**

| solar-powered | ~~climate~~ | energy | region | opportunity |

We have a very sunny ¹ <u>climate</u> in this ² _____ all year round,

so we can use clean forms of ³ _____. Last year, we had the

⁴ _____ to make our home ⁵_____, which is great for us

and the planet!

Use of English: quantifiers

SB p.31

> *Language tip*
> Countable nouns are seen as units, for example, *students, books* and
> *pens*. Uncountable nouns are not seen as units, for example, *work, time* and
> *information*.

1 **Read the examples and complete the headings with *large* or *small*.**

To talk about a ¹ _____ quantity, we use:	To talk about a ² _____ quantity, we use:
a few *children*	a large number of *children*
a small number of *these schools*	many *villages*
a small amount of *time*	a large amount of *information*
a bit of *news*	much *food*

2 **Underline the quantifiers in Activity 1 that we use with countable nouns. Circle the quantifiers we use with uncountable nouns.**

3 **Read and circle.**

1 There were [a large number of / a large amount of] students in the library.

2 The students didn't have [many / much] time during the lesson.

3 There are [many / much] books on your desk.

4 I've got [a few / a small amount of] money to spend today.

5 There's a [large number of / large amount of] information to learn.

Use of English: present perfect

1 **Write sentences using the present perfect.**

1 Sarah can't find her homework. She / lose / it _____She has lost it_____ .

2 Marco fell over. But / he / not hurt himself _____ .

3 There's no juice in the fridge. Anita / drink / it _____ .

4 The children aren't here. They / go out _____ .

5 There's some cake left. Nadia and Ayesha / not finish / it _____ .

2 **Read and match.**

1 I have *just* eaten an ice cream.

2 I haven't eaten an ice cream *yet*.

3 Have you *ever* eaten an ice cream?

4 I have *never* eaten an ice cream.

a I don't know what ice cream is like. I haven't eaten it *at any time in my life up to now*.

b I finished eating an ice cream *a short time ago*.

c There's an ice cream in the freezer. I didn't eat it *at any time up to now*.

d Have you eaten an ice cream *at any time in your life up to now*?

3 **Read and complete the sentences with the present perfect and one of the time adverbs from Activity 2.**

1 Your friend thinks you have finished your dinner and takes your plate.

You say: Wait a minute, I <u>haven't finished yet</u> (not / finish).

2 You drink a big glass of water. Your mother asks, 'Are you thirsty?'

You reply: No, I _____ (have) a glass of water.

3 Your friend has been skateboarding for the first time. She wants to know about you.

She asks: _____ (you / go) skateboarding?

4 You haven't been skateboarding.

You tell your friend: No, I _____ (try) skateboarding.

Listening: setting the scene

SB p.33

Complete the country names and write the continents.

Africa   Asia (×4)   North America

Country	Continent
1 South Africa	Africa
2 B_ng_ad_s_	
3 I_don_si_	
4 C_in_	
5 U_it_d _tat_s o_ Am_ri_a	
6 _ndi_	

Use of English: –ing form as a noun

SB p.34

1 **Unscramble and rewrite the sentences.**

1 is / for / Waiting / train / boring / a

_____

2 really / Daniel / swimming / loves

_____

3 instrument / fun / Learning / is / a / musical

_____

4 stopping / drove / school / We / to / without

_____

5 meeting / friends / her / really / enjoyed / She

_____

2 **Write three sentences of your own using the –ing form as a noun.**

1 _____

_____

2 _____

_____

3 _____

_____

Vocabulary: human rights

Complete the crossword.

Across

3 Right to be _____: nobody can lock you up unless you have broken the law

4 Freedom of _____: you can meet up with other people

6 Right to a _____ life: you don't have to tell anybody about your life at home

Down

1 Freedom of _____: you can go to school

2 Right to own _____: you can enjoy the things you own

5 Freedom of _____: you can say what you think

Check your progress

1 What can you do now?

I can …

understand the main points and specific information in a text ☐

use the present perfect ☐

understand the main points and specific information in a podcast ☐

plan and write about my opinion about schools ☐

design a perfect school ☐

understand and talk about human rights ☐

My learning
What did you learn in this unit?

2 Answer the questions about this unit.

1 What have you enjoyed most?

_____

2 Is there anything you have found difficult?

_____

3 What would you like to learn more about?

_____

4 Bookworms

Listening: vocabulary

SB p.40

Read and complete.

| connection | habits | ~~interview~~ | literature | professor | report |

Tomorrow, I've got an [1] <u>interview</u> at the university with a [2] _____ of American [3] _____. He wrote a [4] _____, which shows a [5] _____ between parent's and children's reading [6] _____.

Use of English: questions with prepositions

SB p.42

Complete the questions with the correct prepositions.

| in | at | to | by | ~~from~~ | of | for | on |

1 <u>From</u> whose point of view is the story told?

2 _____ what time does the reading group begin?

3 _____ which direction is the library?

4 _____ which book is she the author?

5 _____ which book group do you belong?

6 _____ what reason was this book written?

7 _____ what date was the author born?

8 _____ what name is the author best known?

Use of English: sentence adverbs

SB p.42

Read and circle.

1 This book is interesting. I didn't finish it, [though / as well / also].

2 I read the author's first book. I read his second book, [though / either / as well].

3 I like reading fiction. I like reading true stories, [too / either / though].

4 I don't like this author. I don't like that author [also / either / too].

5 The book is very long. [Also / Too / As well], it's not very well written.

Reading: comprehension

SB p.43

1 **Read and circle.**

1 There [are / aren't] enough libraries for all the people living in Bogota.

2 The libraries [are / aren't] in the areas where poor people live.

3 Gutierrez has made a library [but he doesn't like reading / and he loves reading].

4 Gutierrez's [father / mother] loved reading, too.

5 Gutierrez thinks that books are better than [films / e-readers].

2 **Read the text again and answer the questions.**

1 Where does Gutierrez live? _____

2 How many years has he worked as a rubbish collector? _____

3 How many books has he collected? _____

4 How many people live in Bogota? _____

5 How many libraries are there? _____

6 Who are Gutierrez's favourite authors? _____

Reading: thinking about the text

SB p.43

Write three questions of your own about the text. Swap with a partner and answer.

1 Question: _____   Answer: _____

2 Question: _____   Answer: _____

3 Question: _____   Answer: _____

Vocabulary: words in context

SB p.44

Complete the sentences with words from the box.

| invention | community | rescued | luxuries | rubbish |
| afford | e-books | e-reader | | |

1 We can't really _____ to buy _____.

2 How many _____ do you have on your _____?

3 The _____ has come together to clear up the _____ on the beach.

4 The inventor _____ his latest _____ from the fire.

1 **Write the headlines in full sentences. Use the present perfect.**

1 RUBBISH COLLECTOR RESCUES BOOKS FOR COLOMBIAN CHILDREN
  A rubbish collector has rescued some books for some Colombian children.

2 SCIENTISTS DISCOVER TOO MUCH SCREEN TIME BAD FOR CHILDREN

_____

_____

3 FLOODS DESTROY OVER 500 HOMES

_____

2 **Complete the text with words from the box.**

| articles | simple | rules | verbs | perfect | sentences |

* Headlines do not follow the normal ¹ _____ of English grammar

  because they are not written in full ² _____.

* They don't usually include ³ _____ (for example, 'a' or 'the').

* Sometimes, ⁴ _____ can be left out of a sentence – when these are

  used, ⁵ _____ tenses are more common than ⁶ _____ tenses.

3 **In your notebook, write the first paragraph of this article. Answer the five Wh– questions about the article. Who? What? When? Why? Where?**

FLOODS DESTROY OVER 500 HOMES

Use of English: conjunctions of contrast SB p.44

Rewrite the pairs of sentences as one sentence using the word in italics.

1 Most of my friends like digital books. I prefer printed books.   *whereas*
  Most of my friends like digital books, whereas I prefer printed books.

2 The library is small. It has got a lot of books.   *Although*

_____

3 Sam goes to the library every day. It's a long way from his house.   *though*

_____

_____

4 Kelly likes fiction. Jane prefers non-fiction.   *while*

_____

Literature: what makes a good story?

1 **Match words and meanings.**

1 hero	**a** the main character in a book
2 style	**b** the ability to think of a lot of ideas
3 structure	**c** all the facts about something
4 truth	**d** the way in which a story is organised
5 imagination	**e** the way a book is written

2 **Complete the diagram with words from the box.**

> style   characters   ~~ideas~~   structure

good writing
² _____ :
interesting words
and descriptions

interesting
¹ _ideas_: something
that makes you
want to read on

A good story

a clear ⁴ _____: a
beginning, a
middle and an end

realistic ³ _____:
people we care
about

3 **What things do you think make a story a good story and why? Use the ideas from the diagram or your own ideas.**

_____

_____

_____

_____

_____

_____

_____

_____

_____

_____

1 **Find 12 types of books. Match with meanings.**

t	r	a	v	e	l	a	g	z	d	l	f	g	w	d
x	y	z	y	b	q	u	e	s	p	o	r	t	s	v
v	p	m	k	j	r	t	j	c	x	y	s	a	a	q
j	y	c	b	u	o	o	e	i	w	t	q	f	m	k
e	w	h	v	i	m	b	k	e	a	w	h	m	r	v
b	p	k	a	w	a	i	c	n	b	o	q	h	t	q
r	d	e	i	h	n	o	o	c	n	a	t	r	o	l
e	i	g	f	i	c	g	m	e	a	d	h	q	p	d
u	o	m	c	s	e	r	e	f	q	v	o	l	w	f
i	r	r	t	t	a	a	d	i	n	e	r	v	d	c
t	z	b	m	o	n	p	y	c	g	n	r	o	k	y
i	g	g	v	r	k	h	m	t	q	t	o	y	i	e
z	r	k	e	y	f	y	h	i	l	u	r	e	a	e
i	k	x	u	u	i	b	i	o	g	r	a	p	h	y
o	i	p	x	j	p	v	m	n	m	e	i	q	r	z

FICTION

1 <u>romance:</u> a story about people who love each other

2 _____ : a story that is very frightening

3 _____ : a story about something unusual, exciting and perhaps dangerous

4 _____ : a story about something funny

5 _____ : a story about things that happen in the future or in other parts of the universe

NON-FICTION

6 _____ : a story of the life of a person written by another person

7 _____ : the story of your life that you write yourself

8 _____ : a story about a journey to an interesting place

9 _____ : a story about things that happened in the past

10 _____ : a story about sportsmen or sportswomen

Check your progress

1 What can you do now?

I can …

listen to and understand an interview ☐

use questions with prepositions and sentence adverbs ☐

use conjunctions of contrast ☐

talk and write about the advantages and disadvantages of e-readers ☐

understand and talk about literature ☐

2 Answer the questions about this unit.

1 What have you enjoyed most?

_____

2 Is there anything you have found difficult?

_____

3 What would you like to learn more about?

_____

My learning
What did you learn in this unit?

5 Extreme weather

Vocabulary: extreme weather

SB p.52

Read and match.

1 a cold spell		**a** thick cloud that is close to the ground
2 a heat wave		**b** a period of time with low temperatures
3 fog		**c** a long period of time with no rain
4 a drought		**d** when a lot of water covers an area that is usually dry
5 a flood		**e** a period of time with high temperatures
6 a hurricane		**f** a storm with very strong winds and rain

Use of English: present simple passive and past simple passive

SB p.53

1 Complete the sentences in the passive.

1 The thunderstorm _is expected_ (expect) to arrive later today.

2 The house _____ (not flood) at the moment.

3 _____ (people / advise) to stay indoors until the hurricane is over?

4 _____ (elderly people / warn) to take extra care in the heat wave last week.

5 _____ (A severe weather warning / not give) yesterday and it didn't snow.

6 _____ (you / wake up) last night by the storm?

2 Complete the second sentence using the passive.

1 Experts warn drivers only to travel if necessary.
   Drivers _are warned_ only to travel if necessary.

2 Weather forecasters don't expect snow today.

   Snow _____ today.

3 Doctors asked people to check on elderly neighbours during cold spells.

   People _____ to check.

4 Weather forecasters didn't predict the thick fog yesterday morning.

   Thick fog _____ yesterday morning.

5 Teachers advised parents with young children to take extra care during the heat wave.

   Parents with young children _____ to take extra care during the heat wave.

Vocabulary: weather forecasts

1 Read and write the points on the compass.

north	south	east	west	north-west
north-east	south-west	south-east

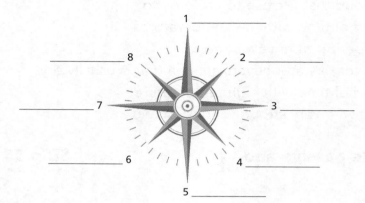

1 _____

2 _____

3 _____

4 _____

5 _____

6 _____

7 _____

8 _____

2 Write the common phrases you will hear in weather forecasts in the correct column of the table below.

difficult / dangerous driving conditions

People are warned to expect …

A severe weather warning was given …

People are advised to …

The storm / fog is expected to clear by …

Allow extra time for journeys and only travel if necessary.

Information about weather	General advice	Advice for drivers
1 _____	3 _____	5 _____
2 _____	4 _____	6 _____

Reading: comprehension

1 **Read the text and write true (T) or false (F). Correct any sentences that are false.**

1 The blogger was woken up by the storm just after midnight. _____

2 He went outside into the garden to watch the storm. _____

3 There was a lot of thunder and lightning. _____

4 He didn't get wet. _____

5 He felt sad when the storm finished. _____

6 Everyone else was woken up by the storm as well. _____

2 **You want to tell your friend about the blog. Describe it in one or two sentences.**
I read this interesting blog today. It was about …

_____

_____

Use of English: adjectives with –*ing* and –*ed* endings

Complete the crossword by reading the clues and making adjectives from the verbs in the box.

| amaze | terrify | exhaust | disappoint | shock |

Across

1 when you feel surprised in a good way

2 when you feel surprised in a bad way

5 something that makes you feel very tired

6 when you feel sad because you didn't get what you had hoped for

7 when you feel very frightened

8 something that makes you feel very frightened

9 something that makes you feel surprised in a bad way

Down

1 something that surprises you in a good way

3 when you feel very tired

4 something that makes you feel sad because you didn't get what you had hoped for

1 across: a m a z e d

Use of English: *this, that, these* and *those*

SB p.55

Choose the correct options.

1 Heavy rain and strong winds are forecast overnight, but you should expect [that / those] to clear by Monday morning.

2 There has been no rain for three months. [This / These] has caused a lot of problems for farmers.

3 [This / These] are the worst storms we've had in years.

4 It will be sunny today, but [that / those] will all change tomorrow when the rain moves in.

Writing: descriptions

SB p.56

1 Imagine that you are standing in the rain in a storm. Complete the sentences.

1 I can see _____.

2 I can hear _____.

3 I can smell _____.

4 I can feel _____.

5 I can taste _____.

2 Use your imagination to rewrite the sentences using similes.

1 The wind was loud.

The wind was as loud as _____.

2 The snow was soft.

The snow was as soft as _____.

3 The lightning is bright.

The lightning is like _____.

4 The storm is strong.

The storm is like _____.

1 **Choose the correct options.**

Text messages are usually [1] [formal / informal]. They [2] [follow / don't follow] the usual rules of grammar and spelling. You [3] [have to / don't have to] use full sentences and you [4] [can / can't] use abbreviations – short ways of writing words. You [5] [have / don't have] to start or finish text messages in any particular way.

2 **Write the text message abbreviations as full sentences.**

1 C u 2mro. _____

2 Lk 4wd 2 it. _____

3 Spk l8tr _____

4 How r u? _____

Check your progress

1 What can you do now?

I can …

listen to and understand a weather forecast ☐

talk about extreme weather ☐

use present simple and past simple passive ☐

read and write a descriptive blog ☐

understand and talk about floods in geography ☐

2 Answer the questions about this unit.

1 What have you enjoyed most?

_____

2 Is there anything you have found difficult?

_____

3 What would you like to learn more about?

_____

My learning

What did you learn in this unit?

6 Extreme planet

Vocabulary: our planet

SB p.62

1 Complete the map with the words from the box.

> Pacific Ocean ×2   Atlantic Ocean ×2   Indian Ocean
> Arctic Ocean   Equator   line of longitude   line of latitude

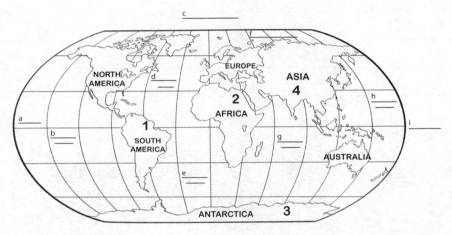

2 Complete the sentences.

1 The best place I've been is _____ because _____ .

2 I want to visit _____ because _____ .

3 I don't want to go to _____ because _____ .

Reading: comprehension

SB p.63

1 Read the text again and match the places to numbers 1–4 on the map above.

> Mount Everest   River Nile   Amazon rainforest   Vostok Station

2 **Read and match.**

1 Mount Everest is
2 Edmund Hilary climbed Mount Everest
3 The River Nile is
4 The Amazon River is
5 The Amazon rainforest is
6 The Pacific Ocean is
7 The hottest temperature on Earth was taken
8 The coldest temperature on Earth was taken

a on 13 September 1922.
b 6.5 million square kilometres.
c 6650 kilometres long.
d in 1953.
e 155 million square kilometres.
f on 21 July 1983.
g 6400 kilometres long.
h 8848 metres high.

3 **Research these questions. Where did you find the answers? Use sources you can trust!**

1 Who was the first woman to climb Mount Everest?
2 Which countries does the Amazon River go through?
3 Approximately, how many plant species live in the Amazon rainforest?
4 What's the largest island in the Pacific Ocean?

4 **Complete the sentences.**

1 The most interesting thing I learned about the Earth today is _____

2 The most surprising thing I learned about the Earth today is _____

3 I would like to find out more about _____ because _____

Vocabulary: extreme adjectives

SB p.64

1 **Find three words that mean *extremely good* and three words that mean *extremely big*. Write them below.**

k	j	p	u	q	e	h	h	k	l	h	d
i	n	c	r	e	d	i	b	l	e	v	q
p	l	q	h	i	f	u	e	k	b	h	x
w	j	k	u	l	q	m	r	i	k	g	m
x	z	u	g	i	g	a	n	t	i	c	h
x	u	z	e	c	p	a	z	q	m	x	f
o	x	n	m	u	n	c	d	m	i	m	s
e	n	o	r	m	o	u	s	v	z	h	w
r	m	a	g	n	i	f	i	c	e	n	t
o	e	i	v	z	i	o	t	j	r	f	i
o	a	u	b	j	u	f	z	g	e	j	p
l	m	a	r	v	e	l	i	o	u	s	d

extremely big
• gigantic
• h_____
• e_____

extremely good
• i_____
• m_____
• m_____

2 Write two sentences using two of the adjectives from Activity 1.

1 _____

2 _____

Vocabulary: words in context

SB p.64

Complete the words.

1 v_l_an_

2 o_e_n

3 p_ak

4 p_pu_at_o_

5 r_i_f_re_t

6 r_c_s

Use of English: adding information with *which, who* and *where*

SB p.65

Complete the text with *which, who* or *where*.

A desert is an extremely dry area, [1]_____ there is less than 250 mm of rain a year. The driest place in the world is the Atacama Desert, [2]_____ is in Chile and Peru. At its centre is a place that scientists call absolute desert, [3]_____ rain has never been recorded. It may be surprising to find out that the Atacama has a population of more than a million people [4]_____ mostly live in the cities near the sea. There are also some farmers, [5]_____ grow olives, tomatoes and cucumbers, in the far north. The night skies, [6]_____ are usually completely clear, make the Atacama Desert one of the best places in the world to look at the stars.

Use of English: adding information with *whose*

SB p.65

1 Look again at this sentence from the text in the Student's Book and choose the correct options.

*This Antarctic station, **whose** winter population is only 13 scientists and engineers, reached a temperature low of –89.2 °C on 21 July 1983.*

The word [1][whose / who's] is used in relative clauses to show possession. It replaces the words [2][he, she, it or they / him, her, it or them / his, her, its or their].

> **Spelling tip**
> Don't confuse the relative pronoun *whose* with *who's* (who is). They sound the same, but the spelling is different.

2 Write one sentence instead of two using a relative clause.

1 Edmund Hillary climbed Mount Everest in 1953. His guide was called Tenzing Norgay.

Edmund Hillary, whose guide was called Tenzing Norgay, climbed Mount Everest

in 1953.

2 The people of the Amazon rainforest have lived there for thousands of years. Their homes are in danger.

3 The scientists in Antarctica live in difficult conditions. Their work is very important.

Vocabulary: useful verbs

SB p.66

1 Replace the underlined phrases in the sentences with the correct form of the verbs from the box.

| disappear | hunt | recycle | destroy |

1 Snakes are being <u>chased and killed</u> for their skin.

2 Many of the monkeys' habitats have <u>gone away</u>.

3 The rainforest is being <u>damaged</u> by tourism.

4 It's important that we <u>use</u> paper <u>again</u>.

Use of English: present continuous passive

Rewrite the sentences in the passive. Only use _by_ if we need to know who did the action of the verb.

1 Something is destroying these bees' habitats.

These bees' habitats are being destroyed.

2 People aren't hunting elephants in this area.

_____

3 The snake is hunting the mouse.

_____

4 People are recycling a lot of paper in this town.

_____

5 Are humans hurting the environment?

_____

Check your progress

1 What can you do now?

I can …

read and talk about extreme places ☐

use non-defining relative clauses ☐

listen to and think about a presentation about extreme animals ☐

talk about and write about my opinion ☐

read an article about an extreme world tour and plan a trip ☐

2 Answer the questions about this unit.

1 What have you enjoyed most?

_____

2 Is there anything you have found difficult?

_____

3 What would you like to learn more about?

_____

My learning

What did you learn in this unit?

Back in time

Vocabulary: talking about history

SB p.74

1 Look and write.

| knight | tomb | mummy | battle |

1

2

3

4

_____ _____ _____ _____

2 Read and match.

1 period
2 Middle Ages

3 site
4 virtual reality
5 exhibition
6 ancient

a a situation produced by a computer that seems almost real
b the period of European history between the end the Roman Empire in 476BCE and about 1500CE.
c an event where interesting things are shown
d a length of time
e very old
f a place where something happens

3 Complete the sentences.

1 My favourite period of history is _____ because _____.

2 If I had a time machine, I would go back to _____

because _____.

Reading: comprehension

SB p.75

Read the texts again. Write _True_ or _False_ or _Doesn't say._

1 Mark went to an exhibition about the Middle Ages. _____
2 Mark learned about King Tutankhamun. _____
3 Tim got a virtual reality app about history for his birthday. _____
4 Tim's app tells you about the famous people who were alive during the Great Fire of London. _____
5 Jan comes from the USA. _____
6 Jan went to visit a historical site last week. _____

Find answers to these questions. Give your sources. Use only sources that you trust!

1 *I want to find out more about Ancient Egypt now. I wonder what sort of people were made into mummies …*

_____

_____

_____

Source: _____

2 *Now, I want to find out more about it, for example, how did the Great Fire of London start?*

_____

_____

_____

Source: _____

3 *I wonder what it was like to be a knight in the Middle Ages …*

_____

_____

_____

Source: _____

Use of English: past continuous passive   SB p.76

Complete the second sentence in the past continuous passive. Use no more than three words.

1 The King was training the knight.

The knight _____ by the King.

2 The fire was burning all the trees in the forest.

All the trees in the forest _____ by the fire.

3 Some people were building a special Middle Ages exhibition when we visited the museum last week.

A special Middle Ages exhibition _____ when we visited the museum last week.

4 People were fighting a big battle when it started to snow.

A big battle _____ when it started to snow.

Use of English: more compound nouns

SB p.76

1 Use one word from each box to make six compound nouns.

~~country~~	back	sun
guide	step	farm

mother	house	~~side~~
book	shine	ground

1 _countryside_

2 _____

3 _____

4 _____

5 _____

6 _____

2 Complete the text with the compound nouns from Activity 1.

Yesterday, I had a lovely day out in the ¹ _countryside_ with my ² _____.

We visited an old ³ _____ and gardens. We bought an interesting

⁴ _____, which told us all about the historical ⁵ _____ of

the house. After we had explored the house, we went for a long walk in the

⁶ _____.

Use of English: past perfect with *never, ever, always* and *already*

SB p.78

Complete the sentences with the correct form of the verbs from the box.

never / see	you / ever / try	already / hear	~~always / think~~

1 We _had always thought_ that King Tutankhamun was just a character in a story.

2 They _____ a real mummy until they went to the exhibition last month.

3 _____ a virtual reality headset before you went to the exhibition?

4 By the time the archaeologist arrived at the site, he _____ the news.

Focus on History: archaeologists' greatest finds

SB pp.80–81

1 **Read and match.**

1 How long was Howard Carter looking for King Tutankhamun's tomb?

2 In what year did Howard Carter find King Tutankhamun's tomb?

3 In what year did King Tutankhamun die?

4 In what year were the ruins of Pompeii found?

5 In what year did a volcano bury the city of Pompeii?

6 How long was Pompeii under the rock?

7 In what year was the Terracotta Army found?

8 In what year was the Terracotta Army made?

9 In what year were the bones of King Richard III found?

10 In what year did King Richard III die?

a c1346 BCE

b 2000 years

c 1485

d 1922

e 209 BCE

f 2013

g 31 years

h 1748

i 79 CE

j 1974

2 **Complete the sentences.**

1 I think that the work done by archaeologists is _____

because _____.

2 I would / wouldn't like to be an archaeologist because _____.

Vocabulary: useful words for talking about history

Complete the crossword

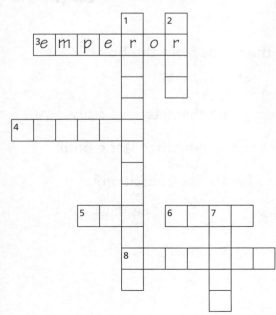

Across

3 a man who rules a group of countries

4 a large model of a person or animal, made of stone or metal

5 to make a hole in the ground

6 to put something in a hole in the ground and cover it up

8 a person in an army

Down

1 a person whose job is to look for and study old things

2 a large group of soldiers who are trained to fight battles on land

7 the parts of a building that remain after something destroys the rest

Check your progress

1 What can you do now?

I can …

read and talk about historical experiences ☐

use the past continuous passive and the past perfect ☐

listen to and think about famous people from the past ☐

read and talk about the work of archaeologists ☐

make a time capsule ☐

2 Answer the questions about this unit.

1 What have you enjoyed most?

_____

2 Is there anything you have found difficult?

_____

3 What would you like to learn more about?

_____

My learning
What did you learn in this unit?

8 Who am I?

Vocabulary: identity and character

SB p.84

1 Match the adjectives to the descriptions.

| warm | calm | generous | confident | independent | creative |

1 I like drawing and painting. I also write my own poems and songs.

_____

2 I am happy to do things on my own and don't need help from others.

_____

3 I give as much money as I can to charity and sometimes I give up my time to clean up rubbish at the beach near my house.

_____

4 People say that I'm very friendly.

_____

5 I'm not shy because I'm sure about my own abilities and ideas.

_____

6 When things get hard, I don't get worried or angry or excited.

_____

2 Find and write the words.

c	h	a	r	a	c	t	e	r	m	h	k
a	u	k	f	n	f	o	s	k	u	h	q
b	i	i	q	a	a	q	j	c	p	g	t
v	i	p	z	t	p	i	i	x	z	i	y
b	o	p	z	i	w	d	c	b	e	y	i
q	q	l	r	o	g	e	n	d	e	r	b
j	p	g	i	n	m	n	q	s	k	i	f
z	d	i	r	a	s	t	c	m	y	x	f
h	h	f	f	l	s	i	m	e	d	i	a
o	x	a	v	i	l	t	i	a	c	t	c
t	u	i	b	t	s	y	x	h	i	l	e
u	r	h	v	y	k	q	p	r	q	u	r

1 _character_: all the things that make you different from other people

2 _____: what makes you who you are

3 _____: belonging to a particular country

4 _____: male or female

5 _____: TV, newspapers, radio, internet and so on

Reading: comprehension

SB p.85

Read the texts again and complete the sentences.

1 Marco grew up in _____ and is proud to be _____ .

2 Saira thinks that men aren't as _____ as women and that women aren't as _____ as men.

3 Lucien's mum is _____ and his dad is _____ .

4 Every day, Arjun reads the _____ on the internet.

5 Kalifa's friends have helped her to feel more _____ at school.

Reading: thinking about the text

SB p.85

1 Which of the people on page 85 of the Student's Book are most similar to you and why?

_____

_____

2 Write your own post to add to the chat room. Talk about who you are and what's important in making your identity.

_____

_____

_____

_____

Use of English: spelling patterns

SB p.86

Correct the spelling mistake in each sentence.

1 I'm not very ~~confidant~~ and feel shy when I meet new people.
         confident

2 Jin is always keen on having new experiances.

3 My brother is very generus and always helps me when he can.

4 The students are independunt and work well on their own.

5 There are a lot of differenses between me and my sister.

6 Sport is an enormouss part of my identity.

Use of English: adjectives + prepositions

1 **Read and match.**

1 proud of	**a** worried
2 amazed at	**b** the same in some ways but not every way
3 keen on / fond of	**c** pleased about something good that you or other people close to you have done
4 similar to	**d** surprised
5 anxious about	**e** like something very much

2 **Complete each sentence with an adjective and preposition.**

1 I'm very <u>fond of</u> going to the cinema. I try to go every week.

2 I feel very _____ _____ my exams. I hope that I do well.

3 I look very _____ _____ my brother. We both have brown eyes and hair.

4 I'm very _____ _____ the goal that I scored today!

5 I was _____ _____ today's news. It was a real surprise.

6 I'm not very _____ _____ fish. I prefer eating meat and vegetables.

3 **Complete the sentences with your own ideas.**

1 I'm very proud of _____.

2 I sometimes feel anxious about _____.

3 I'm very fond of _____.

4 I'm similar to _____.

Use of English: reported speech

SB p.88

1 **Complete the sentences in reported speech. Remember only to change the tense if you need to.**

1 Lucia said, 'I don't like going to the cinema.'

Lucia said that <u>she doesn't like going to the cinema.</u>

2 'These are the books I read on holiday,' said Adam to his sister.

Adam told his sister that _____

3 'We're travelling to Beijing tomorrow,' said Sophia.

Sophia said that _____

4 Aisha said, 'this is where we stayed yesterday.'

Aisha said that _____

5 Robert said, 'I have never been to this restaurant.'

Robert said that _____

2 **Read the conversation. Then complete the text below.**

Reema: Hey, Rachel, [1] **I'm talking** to you from the top of the Eiffel Tower.

Rachel: Really?! Lucky you! [2] **I'm at college** [3] **today**!

Reema: Oh sorry! [4] **We arrived** in Paris [5] **yesterday** and [6] **we're staying** in a lovely hotel [7] **here**. I [8] **haven't been** to France since [9] **last year** and [10] **I'm** happy to be back!

Reema said that [1] <u>she was talking</u> to Rachel from the top of the Eiffel Tower. Rachel

said that [2] _____ at college [3] _____. Reema said

that [4] _____ in Paris [5] _____ and that [6] _____

in a lovely hotel [7] _____. She said that [8] _____ to France

since [9] _____ and that [10] _____ happy to be back.

Focus on Literature: non-fiction

SB pp.90–91

1 **Match the verbs from the text to the meanings.**

1 copy	a not stop
2 pick	b try to do what another person does
3 continue	c choose
4 promise	d form a picture of something in your mind
5 pronounce	e say that you will certainly do something
6 imagine	f make the sound of a word

2 Choose three verbs from Activity 1 and write them in your own sentences.

1 _____ .

2 _____ .

3 _____ .

3 Complete the sentences.

1 I (enjoy / don't enjoy) reading non-fiction books because

_____

_____

2 I (enjoyed / didn't enjoy) reading the extracts from *I Will Always Write Back* because

_____

_____

Check your progress

1 **What can you do now?**

I can …

read and talk about what's important for personal identity ☐

use adjectives + prepositions and reported speech ☐

understand speakers' opinions ☐

check what somebody has said ☐

write an email about myself ☐

2 **Answer the questions about this unit.**

1 What have you enjoyed most?

_____

2 Is there anything you have found difficult?

_____

3 What would you like to learn more about?

_____

My learning

What did you learn in this unit?

Mid-year review

Vocabulary: word hunt

Name four ...

1 types of films

2 people who work in sports

3 countries or continents

4 types of books

5 types of weather

6 ways to describe feelings

7 interesting natural features

8 ways to describe people's character

Vocabulary: a crossword puzzle

Complete the crossword.

Across

1 the person who is against you in a sports competition

4 a long period of time with no rain

5 the environment in which an animal or a plant lives or grows

8 person who studies items from the past, for example, buildings and tools

9 a book or film that is very frightening

Down

2 the story of a film or book

3 a public event where art or interesting objects are shown

6 small metal disc (gold, silver or bronze) you get for doing something good

7 books about people and events that are not real

Writing: punctuation

Read and correct the short story. Add in six missing punctuation marks.

A young girl was sitting in the garden
She was wearing a summer dress
covered in little pink flowers. Suddenly,
a bee, which was making a lot of noise
came and sat on her dress.

"Hello, bee, said the girl.

Hi, flower," replied the bee.

The girl looked at the bee in surprise.

The girl asked, "How can you talk You're only a bee."

"How can you talk? Youre only a flower," replied the bee Then it
flew away.

Vocabulary: using the correct word

Be careful with words that sound the same but mean different things!

1 **Rewrite the sentences correctly.**

  1 Its great to see you.   <u>It's great to see you.</u>

  2 Do you know who's house this is?   _____

  3 I've read all her books accept this one. _____

  4 The Sahara is the biggest dessert in the world. _____

  5 We could of gone to school today.   _____

  6 Did you loose your phone again?   _____

2 **Write sentences using these words.**

  1 **a** bee _____

    b be _____

  2 **a** warn _____

    b worn _____

  3 **a** scene _____

    b seen _____

Power of music

Read the blog again and choose the correct option.

1 Why does the blogger think that music can be a very powerful art form?
  a Because music can be quiet.   **b** Because music can be loud.
  c Because music can be exciting.

2 What did Band Aid do?
  a They made a song that helped some people.
  b They made a song that helped the Arctic.
  c They made a song that built schools for Emmanuel Jal.

3 Why did Ludovico write music about the Arctic?
  a Because he wanted to make money.   **b** Because he wanted to visit the Arctic.
  c Because he wanted to make people care about the Arctic.

Reading: research   SB p.100

Find out more about these items mentioned in the blog. Give your sources, too. Remember only to use sources that you trust.

1 *Their song made a lot of noise and also made a lot of money to help people in Africa.*
Find out more about Band Aid. Who was involved? What did they do to help? What were the results of what they did?

_____

_____

Source: _____

2 *Ludovico Einaudi wanted to make people care about the fact that the Arctic is in danger.*
Find out more about why the Arctic is in danger. What are people doing about it? How has Ludovico Einaudi's music helped?

_____

_____

Source: _____

3 *Emmanuel Jal has now helped a lot of charities.*
Find out about what charities Emmanuel Jal has helped. In what ways has he used his music to help other people?

_____

_____

Source: _____

Vocabulary: words in context

SB p.102

Complete the text with the correct form of the words from the box.

| issue | survive | perform | charity | pay attention | environmental |

Music makes people ¹ _____ to important ² _____ and

social ³ _____ . For example, last month musicians ⁴ _____ a

concert to support a local ⁵ _____ . They made a lot of money to help people

who ⁶ _____ last year's hurricane.

Use of English: verbs + prepositions

SB p.102

1 Complete the sentences with the correct form of the verbs from the box + *about or with*.

| disagree | care | ~~share~~ | complain | dream | communicate |

1 I don't have my own computer – this is the computer I <u>share with</u> my sister.

2 He _____ the environment – it's very important to him.

3 My parents have different opinions to me – I _____ them.

4 Our teacher is good at telling us information – he _____ us very well.

5 I _____ moving to the USA – I really hope it happens one day.

6 Sarah's soup was cold – she _____ it and the waiter brought her another bowl.

2 Complete the sentences with the correct preposition and your own ideas.

1 I dream _____ .

2 I care _____ .

3 I disagree _____ .

Use of English: who, which/that, where, when, why

SB p.102

Complete the sentences with the correct relative pronoun.

1 This is the town <u>where</u> we used to live.

2 People _____ don't like children shouldn't be teachers.

3 My grandparents live in Spain. That's _____ I moved here.

4 It was summer _____ we went to the beach.

5 The car is a form of transport _____ is bad for the environment.

Use of English: whose

SB p.102

1 Look at this sentence from the blog and complete the grammar rule.

*Think about the people **whose** lives we can change.*

We use the word *whose* in defining relative clauses as:

a an object pronoun

b a subject pronoun

c a possessive pronoun

2 Complete the sentences with *who* or *whose*.

1 I met a girl _____ mother works at our school.

2 I met a girl _____ used to go to our school.

3 Simon and Jerome are the boys _____ visited me last week.

4 Simon and Jerome are the boys _____ ball I found in the garden.

5 This is the woman _____ sister is on TV.

6 This is the woman _____ is on TV.

Vocabulary: feelings

SB p.103

Complete the sentences with the adjectives from the box.

| relaxed | stressed | lonely | miserable | embarrassed | cheerful |

1 I feel very _____ because I have a test tomorrow and I really want to

do well. After the test is over, I'll feel _____ because I'll have nothing to worry about!

2 Guyaume was very unhappy last week – he was _____ because his cat was

missing. But today the cat came home and he's very _____ again.

3 I felt very _____ on the bus today because I didn't have anyone to talk

to. Then I fell over when I was getting off the bus in front of lots of people and that

made me feel _____.

Use of English: reported questions

SB p.104

Complete the table with direct and reported questions.

Direct question	Reported question
He asked me, "Where do you come from?"	**1** <u>He asked me where I came from.</u>
2 _____	She asked if I would help her.
Sarah asked Dominic, "Are you learning the piano or the guitar?"	**3** _____
4 _____	Janie asked her friend what her favourite song was.
Mark asked his mother, "did you see my music homework yesterday?"	**5** _____
6 _____	Pierre asked his cousin whether he preferred classical music or pop music.

Writing: punctuation

SB p.104

1 Read the *Punctuation tip* and add the missing punctuation into the sentences below.

  1 What time does your music lesson start she asked her friend

  2 They asked their teacher Are we going to play in the school concert

  3 Did you practise this song Janus asked his friend

  4 What's your favourite instrument he asked Bader

> **Punctuation tip**
>
> Note the position of commas and question marks in the following direct questions.
>
> *"What do you want to listen to?" Otis asked his friend.*
>
> *He asked them, "Do you listen to the radio or MP3 player?"*

2 Write these reported questions as direct questions. Remember to use the correct punctuation.

  1 He asked me what time I would be home.

  <u>"What time will you be home?" he asked me.</u>

  2 Kim asked her sister if she wanted a drink.

  _____

3 Leo asked Mina where his coat was.

_____

4 Sophie asked her friend whether she was cold.

_____

Focus on Music: instrument families in an orchestra

SB p.106

Write the instrument name and family it belongs to.

1

2

3

4

tuba, brass   _____   _____   _____   _____   _____   _____

5

6

7

8

_____   _____   _____   _____   _____   _____   _____   _____

Check your progress

1 What can you do now?

I can …

read and talk about the power of music ☐

use defining relative clauses and reported questions ☐

understand speakers' opinions ☐

talk and write about whether music is important ☐

talk about the instruments in an orchestra ☐

2 Answer the questions about this unit.

1 What have you enjoyed most?

_____

2 Is there anything you have found difficult?

_____

3 What would you like to learn more about?

_____

My learning
What did you learn in this unit?

Vocabulary: useful adjectives

SB p.110

Complete the sentences with the adjectives from the box.

local	knowledgeable	lively
experienced	peaceful	convenient

1 My cousin knows a lot about the history and culture of the city – he is

very _____ about it.

2 We stayed in a quiet hotel in the country – it was very _____.

3 The hotel is very _____ because it's near the centre of town and the train station.

4 We don't want to go far from the hotel – do you know any good _____ restaurants?

5 This area is very _____ – there are two theatres, a cinema and a lot of restaurants and cafes.

6 The tour guide has been doing his job for 20 years – he's very _____.

Use of English: reported commands

SB p.111

Rewrite the sentences in bold as reported commands.

Tara: ¹ **Look at this article!** There's a new exhibition at the museum.

Laura: Oh yes, it looks good. Shall we go on Saturday?

Tara: No, I can't. I'm going away on Friday.

Laura: Oh yes. ² **Don't forget to send me a postcard!** We could go when you get back.

Tara: ³ **Don't worry about me.** I don't really want to go anyway. ⁴ **Go with Sarah.**

Laura: OK, I'll give her a ring. ⁵ **Pass me the phone.**

1 Tara told Laura to look at that article.

2 _____

3 _____

4 _____

5 _____

Use of English: *have/get something done*

SB p.111

Complete the sentences with *have* or *get something done*.

1 <u>I had my car fixed</u> (I / my car / fix) yesterday.

2 _____ (you / house / clean) last week?

3 _____ (The actor / always / hair / do) when he goes out.

4 _____ (They / their house / build) last year.

5 _____ (they / pizza / deliver) last night?

6 _____ (my grandmother / ears / test) last week.

Vocabulary: a great city

SB p.112

1 **Match.**

1 lively, exciting	a architecture
2 plenty of job	b culture
3 interesting, friendly	c system
4 beautiful, original	d people
5 reliable transport	e spaces
6 parks and open	f opportunities

2 **Answer the questions.**

1 Which of these things do you think is most important in a city? Why?

_____

2 Which of these things do you think is least important in a city? Why?

_____

Reading: thinking about the text

SB p.113

1 Read the three tweets about the article. Which do you think describes it best?

Tweet
@tweet
Follow

Interesting survey about why people who live in cities are happier than people in the country.

Tweet
@tweet
Follow

Great read about the five most important cities in the world.

Tweet
@tweet
Follow

Check out this article about what people look for in great cities.

2 Think about the survey results by answering questions about the place where you live.

1 Does the place you live have a lively culture? Why? Why not?

_____

2 What sort of job opportunities are there?

_____

3 What's your favourite open space and why?

_____

4 Is there a reliable transport system? Why? Why not?

_____

5 Are there interesting, friendly people?

_____

Vocabulary: useful nouns

SB p.113

Find and correct six spelling mistakes.

I read a report that said that it's important to get away from the stres of city life sometimes and that this can have great health benifits. So, last week, I took some time out of my busy day to go to an exibition at a local art galery. As I was looking at a picture, I realised that a stranjer was waving at me from the other side of the room. He was some distanse away from me and I didn't recognise him. As he came closer, I realised that it was my old art teacher from school! We were happy to see each other again and looked at the pictures together!

_____   _____

_____   _____

_____   _____

Use of English: infinitives after adjectives and verbs

SB p.114

1 **Match the words with a similar meaning.**

1 shocked	**a** seem
2 likely	**b** surprised
3 certain	**c** sure
4 appear	**d** probable
5 continue	**e** wait to happen
6 expect	**f** not stop

2 **Put the words in the correct order to make sentences.**

1 shocked / brother. / was / to / The / see / girl / her

_____

2 to / at / We / arrive / 3 o'clock. / expect

_____

3 appears / open. / The / art gallery / to / be

_____

4 by / The / train. / students / travel / continued / to

_____

5 until / Are / Friday? / you / to / likely / stay

_____

6 arrive / post / tomorrow. / The / in / letter / certain / is / to / the

_____

Use of English: noun phrases

SB p.114

Use your imagination to think of interesting noun phrases.

1 The boy moved to the city.
The <u>boy in my book</u> moved to <u>the lively, charming, new city with a lot of interesting</u> <u>culture.</u>

2 The fox ran through the park.

_____

3 The bus crossed the bridge.

_____

4 The student worked in the library.

_____

Focus on the World: The best cities in the world

SB pp.116–117

1 **Match the cities to the countries.**

1 Munich   a Austria

2 Vienna   b New Zealand

3 Auckland   c Switzerland

4 Vancouver   d Germany

5 Zurich   e Canada

2 **Complete these things that make a difference to the quality of life in a city.**

☐ p_lit_cs   ☐ tra_spo_t

☐ ec_no_ics   ☐ c_ltu_e

☐ soc_al free_om   ☐ sh_ps

☐ heal_h ce_tres   ☐ h_use_

☐ ed_cati_n   ☐ nat_ral en_iron_ent

3 **Look again at the things in Activity 2. Number them from 1 (*most important*) to 10 (*least important*) when it comes to the quality of your life.**

Check your progress

1 What can you do now?

I can …

talk and write about city and country life   ☐

use reported commands and *have / get something done*   ☐

understand the detail of speakers' and writers' arguments   ☐

give a presentation about my favourite city   ☐

write a description of my favourite city   ☐

2 Answer the questions about this unit.

1 What have you enjoyed most?

_____

2 Is there anything you have found difficult?

_____

3 What would you like to learn more about?

_____

My learning

What did you learn in this unit?

A job for life

Reading: comprehension

SB p.122

Read the text again and write *True, False* or *Doesn't Say*. Correct any sentences that are false.

1 Nurses are happier than doctors in their jobs._____
2 People who earn a lot of money are happier than those who don't. _____
3 Farmers are happier than lawyers._____
4 The teacher thinks that children are amusing and clever. _____
5 The nurse doesn't mind working long hours. _____
6 The doctor doesn't work with other people very often. _____

Reading: research

SB p.122

Find out more about one of the jobs mentioned in the article. Give your sources. Remember only to use sources that you trust. Find out:

* how you learn to do this job

* what a typical day is like.

_____

_____

_____

Sources: _____

Vocabulary: multi-word verbs with *put*

SB p.123

Complete the multi-word verbs with *put*.

1 Could you put the washing machine _____, please.

2 The firefighter put the fire _____ quickly.

3 Could you put me _____ to Mr Harris, please?

4 I've put all the boxes _____ in the cupboard for you.

5 My teacher put the exam _____ until next week because we missed a lesson.

6 I put my suitcase _____ while I was standing in the queue.

Vocabulary: jobs

1 Read and match.

| designer | lawyer | scientist | vet | musician | firefighter |

1 _____

2 _____

3 _____

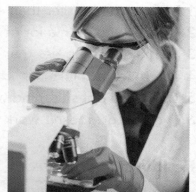

4 _____

5 _____

6 _____

2 Write a sentence to describe what these people do.

1 A designer _____

2 A lawyer _____

3 A scientist _____

4 A vet _____

5 A musician _____

6 A firefighter _____

3 Complete the sentences about the jobs from Activity 1.

1 I think the most interesting job is a _____ because _____.

2 I think the most important job is a _____ because _____.

3 I would most like to become a _____ because _____.

Vocabulary: talking about jobs

SB p.125

1 Replace the underlined words in the text with the words from the box.

part-time job   salary   training   career   work experience

I'm still not sure what I want do to as my <u>job in life</u> ¹ _____. Last week, I did some <u>work for a company for a short period of time to see if I liked it</u> ² _____ at a hospital. I will have to do many years of <u>learning about how to do the job</u> ³ _____ if I want to be a doctor. I might get a <u>job where I work for part of each week</u> ⁴ _____ and the <u>money that I earn from the job</u> ⁵ _____ can go towards my studies.

2 Answer the questions.

1 What *training* do you need to do to follow the *career* you want?

_____

2 Where would you like to do *work experience* and why?

_____

3 If you could have any *part-time job* in the world, what would you choose and why?

_____

4 Is a good *salary* important to you in a job?

_____

Use of English: asking questions politely

SB p.126

Rewrite the questions to make them more polite.

1 What time does the shop close?

Do you know _____

2 When can you start work experience?

Could _____

3 What's the company name?

I wonder _____

4 Is the station this way?

Could _____

5 Is there a bank near here?

I wonder _____

Use of English: using modal verbs

1 Read and choose the correct option below.

Lynn: Dad, I've got my first day of work experience tomorrow – ¹_____ you give me some tips?

Dad: Of course. You ²_____ wear jeans, that's for sure. It ³_____ be OK to wear casual clothes for some jobs, but you ⁴_____ always try to look smart for work experience.

Lynn: Dad, ⁵_____ you drive me tomorrow? I ⁶_____ be late if I take the train.

Dad: Yes, of course

Lynn: Thanks Dad.

1 a should **b** may not **c** could **d** might not

2 a might **b** would **c** may not **d** shouldn't

3 a may not **b** might **c** shouldn't **d** would

4 a should **b** may **c** might not **d** could

5 a shouldn't **b** would **c** may not **d** wouldn't

6 a should **b** might **c** may not **d** wouldn't

2 Use a modal verb to complete the second sentence so that it means the same as the first.

1 It's possible that I will get a job over the summer.
I _____ get a job over the summer.

2 It would be a good idea if I wear smart clothes.
I _____ wear smart clothes.

3 It would be a bad idea for you to give up the piano.
You _____ give up the piano.

Focus on Maths: analysing data

Across

2 the number that is in the middle of a set of numbers

3 the number that appears most often in a set

5 the difference between the lowest and highest number in a set

8 the word for ×

Down

1 the word for ÷

2 the result of adding a set of numbers together and dividing them by the number of things

4 the word for −

6 the word for +

7 the word for =

Check your progress

1 What can you do now?

I can …

listen to and take part in a job interview ☐

use modal verbs, polite questions and multi-word verbs ☐

talk about and write a description of my dream job ☐

work out the mean, median, mode and range in maths ☐

carry out a survey and analyse the data ☐

2 Answer the questions about this unit.

1 What have you enjoyed most?

_____

2 Is there anything you have found difficult?

_____

3 What would you like to learn more about?

_____

My learning
What did you learn in this unit?

12 Helping hand

Vocabulary: charity and kindness

SB p.132

1 Complete the text with the words in the box.

> charity   kindness   duty   care   stranger   involved

I think it's our ¹ _____ to our community to give something back and

show the people around us that we ² _____ . So, I decided to get

³ _____ in a local ⁴ _____ . For the last three months, I've been

helping out at the local food bank, which hands out food parcels to people who need

them. Showing a bit of ⁵ _____ to a ⁶ _____ always makes my day.

2 Answer the questions.

1 Do you think it's our duty to show people we care? Why? Why not?

_____

2 Are you involved in any local charities? Would you like to be? Give details.

_____

3 How do you feel when you show kindness to a stranger?

_____

Use of English: using modal verbs

SB p.133

1 Complete the sentences with *must, have to, mustn't* or *don't have to*.

1 We have a school uniform – we _____ wear our own clothes to school.

2 I strongly suggest you listen – you _____ pay attention.

3 We aren't allowed to leave our bikes here – we _____ move them.

4 You can decide what you want to do – you _____ come with us.

5 You need to stay in bed until you're better – you _____ get up.

6 We're late – we _____ leave now.

2 Choose the correct options.

1 I strongly believe in helping people. We [must / don't have to] show others that we care.

2 You aren't allowed coffee in the classroom. You [must / mustn't] drink it in here.

3 It's up to you whether you order a suspended coffee. You [have to / don't have to] buy one.

4 We need to clear away our cups. We [have to / don't have to] leave the kitchen tidy.

Reading: comprehension

SB p.134

Read the text again and match questions and answers.

1 How does the environmental charity protect forests?

2 What types of animals does the animal charity rescue?

3 What does the animal charity do to people who are unkind to animals?

4 Why do art workshops help people who can't talk?

5 What does the arts charity help people to do through drama?

6 What does sport do in divided communities?

a It reports them to the police.

b It helps them to find a voice.

c It stops people cutting them down and plants new trees.

d It helps them to find hope after difficult experiences.

e It brings people together.

f Animals that are in danger.

Reading: research

SB p.134

Write about a charity that you would like to support. Find out what it does and what its main aims are. Complete the box and remember to use the correct punctuation for bullet points.

Name: _____

This charity _____

- _____

- _____

- _____

- _____

Punctuation: bullet points

SB p.135

Write the missing punctuation in this text.

Lists are useful because

    we can write lots of different ideas

    they make us check we aren't saying the same thing twice

    they are easy to read

Vocabulary: charity work

SB p.135

Complete the crossword with the missing words from the sentences. What is the vertical word in the grey boxes and what does it mean?

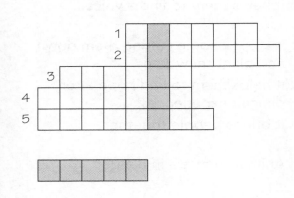

1 Everyone should be able to use libraries – we should all have a_____ to them.

2 We tried to p_____ the injured bird and keep it safe until we got to the vet.

3 The firefighter tried to r_____ the cat, which was stuck up a tree.

4 The city is d_____ and the two parts are quite different.

5 They are building a new classroom for d_____ children, which will have facilities that are specially designed for their needs.

Use of English: pronouns *somebody, nothing, anyone, ...*

SB p.135

1 Complete the table with the missing pronouns.

	–one	–body	–thing
every–	1 _____	2 _____	everything
some–	3 _____	somebody	4 _____
any–	anyone	5 _____	6 _____
no–	7 _____	8 _____	nothing

2 Complete the sentences with one of the pronouns from Activity 1.

1 I really want to do _____ to help out at my local food bank.

2 Is there _____ here who can volunteer on Saturday?

3 _____ cares about these animals any more so they are dying out.

4 We are all doing _____ we possibly can to help.

5 Sam wanted to help his friend move house, but there was _____ for him to do, so he went home.

6 _____ in the school took part in the race for charity and they raised a lot of money.

Use of English: adverbs

SB p.136

1 **Read and complete the spelling rules for adverbs.**

| change the *e* to *y*   change the *y* to *i*   keep the *y*   add *–ly* |

1 We usually [1] _____ to an adjective to make an adverb.

quick = quickly   usual = usually   immediate = immediately

2 When an adjective ends in a consonant + *le* (*–ble, –ple, –tle, –gle, –dle, –kle*), we [2] _____ to make an adverb.

gentle = gently   possible = possibly   simple = simply

3 When an adjective ends in a *y*, we [3] _____ if it's more than one syllable, but [4] _____ in one-syllable words.

easy = easily   happy = happily   shy = shyly

2 **Complete the sentences by making adverbs from the adjectives in the box.**

| slow   angry   terrible   sleepy   cheap |

1 The driver shouted at us _____ when we kicked a ball into his car.

2 You must drive _____ in this area because there are a lot of pedestrians.

3 They lived very _____ when they were travelling and spent hardly any money.

4 The children behaved _____ in the restaurant and their mother took them home.

5 He got out of bed _____ because he hadn't slept much the night before.

3 **Write the adverbs from the box in the correct part of the table below.**

| later   frequently   here   normally   occasionally   already everywhere   immediately   nearby   recently   usually   away |

Where?	When?	How often?
• _____	• _____	• _____
• _____	• _____	• _____
• _____	• _____	• _____
• _____	• _____	• _____

4 **Choose an adverb from each column and use it in a sentence.**

1 Where? _____

2 When? _____

3 How often? _____

1 **Write the abstract nouns next to the correct definitions.**

friendship   strength   courage   character   greatness

1 _____ : the quality someone shows when they are not afraid

2 _____ : all the things that make a person different from other people

3 _____ : something that makes someone very important

4 _____ : a relationship between two or more friends

5 _____ : how strong you are

2 **Answer the questions.**

1 What did you enjoy about reading the extracts from *Wonder*?

_____

2 What did you learn from reading the extracts from *Wonder*?

_____

3 Would you like to read the rest of the book? Why? Why not?

_____

3 **Complete the sentences.**

This week, I'm going to be kind at school by _____

I'm going to be kind at home by _____

Check your progress

1 **What can you do now?**

I can …

listen to a podcast about being kind to other people ☐

use modal verbs, adverbs and pronouns ☐

read about different charities and talk about which one to support ☐

write a letter to my head teacher about my chosen charity ☐

do a kindness project to make the world a better place ☐

2 **Answer the questions about this unit.**

1 What have you enjoyed most?

2 Is there anything you have found difficult?

3 What would you like to learn more about?

My learning
What did you learn in this unit?

Reading: understanding specific information

SB p.145

Read the blog again and match.

1 When she checked Facebook,

a she was disappointed that nobody had replied to her tweet.

2 When she checked Twitter,

3 When she checked Instagram,

b she is a smartphone addict.

c she was upset that nobody had commented on her video of a cat.

4 She admits that

5 She tried to give up her phone, but

d she wasn't very successful.

e she was sad about a party that she hadn't been invited to.

Reading: comprehension

SB p.145

Answer the questions.

1 Do you think it's a good idea to check social media before you get up in the morning? Why? Why not?

_____

2 Are you nomophobic? Do you know anyone who is nomophobic? Are you addicted to any other form of technology?

_____

3 Were you surprised by the results of the report mentioned in the text? Why? Why not?

_____

4 Have you ever tried to give up some form of technology? What happened? Would you like to try?

_____

Punctuation: possessives

SB p.145

Add the missing apostrophes.

1 I have two brothers who share a computer. This is my brothers computer.
   I have two brothers who share a computer. This is my brothers' computer.

2 I have one brother who has his own computer. This is my brothers computer.

3 This phone belongs to the girl. This is the girls phone.

4 This office belongs to our head teacher. The head teachers office is large.

5 All the students did very well in the exam. The students exam results were very good.

Vocabulary: social media

1 Choose the correct option to complete the sentences.

1 When you _____ something, you take some form of information that someone else has posted and you make it visible to all of your friends or the people who follow you.

   a share   **b** comment   **c** update

2 When you _____ information or a photo, you put it online so that other people can see it.

   a comment   **b** post *or* upload   **c** update

3 When you _____ on something on a social media site, you add to the conversation.

   a post   **b** comment   **c** share

4 On Twitter you can _____ your own message and you can _____ other people's messages.

   a share / comment on   **b** tweet / retweet   **c** like / update

5 When you _____ something on social media, you are saying that you think something is good.

   a like   **b** comment   **c** upload

6 When you _____ a website or status, you add the latest information.

   a like   **b** comment   **c** update

2 All the verb options in Activity 1 can also be used as nouns. Look at the example below using *share*. Choose four more verbs from Activity 1 and write sentences using them as nouns.

Example: My photo of a funny fish got 123 shares!

1 _____

2 _____

3 _____

4 _____

3 Read and match.

1 Facebook   **a** is a social media site where users share photographs, which are deleted as soon as they are viewed.

2 Twitter   **b** is mainly a video-sharing social media site.

3 Instagram   **c** is a social media site where users create profiles, upload photos and videos, send messages and keep in touch with friends.

4 Snapchat   **d** is mainly a photo-sharing social media site.

5 YouTube   **e** is a social media site where users post short messages of 140 characters or less.

Use of English: talking about regrets

SB p.146

1 **Read the first sentence. Then, complete the second sentence to show regret.**

1 I haven't got my phone, so I can't call my mum.

I wish _____ my phone.

2 Mario didn't take any photographs and now he feels sad about it.

If only _____ some photographs.

3 The students forgot their passwords and couldn't do their work.

The students shouldn't _____ their passwords.

4 I didn't help my sister and now I feel bad.

I should _____ my sister.

5 I went to bed very late last night, so I'm really tired.

I wish _____ so late last night.

6 You missed the presentation, so you can't do the homework.

If only _____ the presentation.

2 **Complete the sentences with your own ideas.**

1 I'm tired – I wish _____

2 I didn't study for this exam – I should _____

3 You're late for school – you shouldn't _____

4 The shop is closed now – if only I _____

3 **Write three things that you regret doing or not doing.**

1 _____

2 _____

3 _____

Find six abstract nouns in the wordsearch. Write them next to the definitions below.

s	r	t	t	u	s	m	o	k	x	v
h	a	p	p	i	n	e	s	s	s	i
n	a	z	t	r	e	c	u	f	a	d
v	v	e	t	z	l	o	c	r	b	l
o	p	p	o	r	t	u	n	i	t	y
s	z	a	r	t	y	h	v	a	v	e
x	o	n	x	t	h	o	u	g	h	t
s	d	p	d	a	n	g	e	r	g	s
h	w	i	s	a	d	n	e	s	s	s
e	y	n	b	s	u	c	c	e	s	s
s	z	o	y	r	o	v	c	u	o	q

1 <u>thought</u>: an idea or opinion

2 _____: when you do well and get the result you wanted

3 _____: something that can hurt or harm you

4 _____: a situation in which it is possible for you to do something you want to do

5 _____: a feeling of pleasure or satisfaction

6 _____: a feeling of unhappiness

Use of English: multi-word verbs

SB p.148

Complete the sentences with the correct form of *give* + a preposition from the box below.

| in (×2)   away   out   up   ~~back~~ |

1 Denita <u>gave back</u> my scarf, which she had borrowed.

2 The students _____ their essays tomorrow.

3 They _____ free coffees in the shopping centre today, so we didn't have to pay!

4 Rita _____ and agreed to go to the concert last weekend even though she didn't really want to.

5 I _____ chocolate for three months last year – I really missed it!

6 Will you please _____ the books to all the students, Hannah?

Focus on ICT

SB p.150

1 Complete the definitions with words from the box below.

| personal   click   password   phishing   identity |
| privacy   cyberbullying   junk   spam   virus |

1 _____ on a link: use your mouse to press on a highlighted word or icon on the screen, which will take you to another website

2 _____ information, for example, your email address, mobile phone number or date of birth

3 _____ settings: controls you set up online to say who can look at information about you

4 _____ folder: a part of your email system where spam emails are sent

5 _____ emails: emails (usually trying to sell you something or click on a link) that are sent to you even though you haven't asked for them

6 _____ theft: steal someone's personal information and use it to get money illegally

7 _____: when someone is unkind or tells lies about someone online.

8 _____: a program that enters a computer system and changes or destroys the information that is there

9 _____: a secret word or phrase that allows you to use a computer system

10 _____: emails that try to get you to reveal personal information and passwords

2 **Write three things you can do to help you to stay safe online.**

1 _____

2 _____

3 _____

Check your progress

My learning
What did you learn in this unit?

1 What can you do now?

I can …

understand a blog about mobile phone addiction	☐
talk about regrets and use abstract nouns and multi-word verbs	☐
talk and write about the advantages and disadvantages of growing up in the digital age	☐
stay safe online	☐
talk about digital footprints	☐

2 Answer the questions about this unit.

1 What have you enjoyed most?

_____

2 Is there anything you have found difficult?

_____

3 What would you like to learn more about?

_____

14 Advertising

Reading: comprehension
SB pp.154–155

Read the signs again and correct the mistakes in these sentences. One sentence is already correct.

Sign one: There's a special offer today for $2.99.

_____

Sign two: There are bigger reductions on beds than there are on sofas.

_____

Sign three: This sale is on clothes from the new season.

_____

Sign four: This sale is happening on a Tuesday.

_____

Sign five: You can buy one suitcase, but pay for two.

_____

Writing: shop signs
SB pp.154–155

Read the situations and write signs for each shop. Use expressions from the signs in the Student's book.

1 Electronics shop: 10% off mobile phones

2 Bed shop: closing down sale

Vocabulary: sales
SB pp.154–155

Find words on the signs that have the following meanings.

Sign one **1** a price that is lower than it usually is: _special offer_

Sign two **2** a reduction in the usual price of something: _____

3 another word for a shop: _____

4 an adjective that means small in size or number: _____

Sign three **5** a word that means an arrangement of things in a shop: _____

6 when something is made smaller or less than it was before: _____

Sign five **7** when a shop stops working as a business: _____

8 a word that means the total amount of goods that a shop has available to sell: _____

Use of English: talking about quantity

1 **Look and write.**

1

two loaves of b_____

2

one item of c_____

3

one carton of j_____

4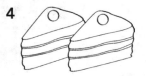

two slices of c_____

5

three bars of c_____

6

one piece of f_____

2 **Choose the correct options.**

1 Could I have two _____ of tea, please?
   a cups   **b** bars   **c** loaves

2 There's a _____ of milk in the fridge.
   a slice   **b** piece   **c** bottle

3 I'd like four _____ of bread, please.
   a bottles   **b** slices   **c** bars

4 Do we need a _____ of orange juice?
   a bar   **b** piece   **c** carton

5 Could you pass me a _____ of paper, please?
   a piece   **b** slice   **c** bar

6 Would you like a _____ of chocolate?
   a loaf   **b** bottle   **c** bar

3 **Correct the spelling mistakes below. One sentence is already correct.**

1 I have lost two scarfs this year. _____

2 The thiefs escaped out of the window. _____

3 I've put up some new shelfs. _____

4 The roofs on these houses are old. _____

5 I cleared up the leaves from the path. _____

6 I saw two wolfs in the forest. _____

4 Write three sentences using words from the box. Use your imagination.

slice   piece   item   bar   loaf   carton

1 _____

2 _____

3 _____

Vocabulary: useful expressions for sales

SB p.156

Choose the correct prepositions to complete the signs.

Come and see what we have ¹[in / on] sale!
15% ²[under / off] all shoes!! Many items of clothing
³[in / at] half price!

Hundreds of special offers ⁴[in / into] store today!!
Cartons of milk: two ⁵[at / for] the price ⁶[of / on] one

New furniture ⁷[on / in] stock now! Sofas ⁸[down by / down in] 10%!
Come and see what we have ⁹[in / on] display!

Vocabulary: advertising

SB p.157

Match words and definitions.

1 taste (n)   a something you make or grow in order to sell it
2 influence (n)   b affect what someone does or what happens.
3 product (n)   c give all your attention to
4 focus on (v)   d grow or change over a period of time
5 encourage (v)   e give someone hope or confidence
6 develop (v)   f someone's choice in all the things they like or buy

Use of English: *so that, in order to, to*

Review the examples in the box. Then write one sentence instead of two using the words in brackets.

Positive	
I went online	**in order to** do some research for science.
	to do some shopping.
	so that I could chat with my friends.

Negative	
I ran fast	**in order not to** miss the bus.
	so as not to be late for school.
	so that I didn't come last in the race.

1 I moved to Spain. I wanted to learn Spanish. (*in order to*)
   I moved to Spain in order to learn Spanish.

2 I joined a new social media website. I wanted to chat to friends. (*to*)

_____

3 Lisa exercises every day. She wants to stay healthy. (*so that*)

_____

4 The boys are studying very hard. They don't want to fail their exams. (*in order not to*)

_____

5 I put on a jumper. I didn't want to be cold. (*so as not to*)

_____

6 I put the appointment in my phone. I didn't want to forget about it. (*so that*)

_____

Use of English: compound adjectives

SB p.158

Complete the sentences with compound adjectives from the box.

fast-changing	thousand-dollar	15-year-old	~~middle-aged~~
	up-to-date	30-second	

1 My parents are in their forties. They are <u>middle-aged</u> people.

2 This website changes very fast. It's a _____ website.

3 This car cost thousands of dollars. It's a _____ car.

4 This advert lasts 30 seconds. It's a _____ advert.

5 I've got the new phone that has just been released. It's an _____ phone.

6 My brother is 15. He's a _____ boy.

Read the article again and answer the questions.

1 Why did people get excited about the photograph of the bird in South Africa?

_____

2 What did the video that was posted by BirdLife South Africa reveal?

_____

3 What sort of art do the artists of Washed Ashore make?

_____

4 What do they use to make this art?

_____

5 What did David Walliams do to raise awareness and money for charity?

_____

6 What did the flash mob in China teach people?

_____

Check your progress

My learning
What did you learn in this unit?

1 **What can you do now?**

I can …

understand shop signs ☐

talk about quantities, use *so that*, *in order to*, *to* and compound adjectives ☐

talk about adverts and advertising ☐

write a product review ☐

make my own advertisement ☐

2 **Answer the questions about this unit.**

1 What have you enjoyed most?

_____

2 Is there anything you have found difficult?

_____

3 What would you like to learn more about?

_____

Reading: comprehension

SB pp.166–167

1 Read the article again and complete the table.

	Raymond Wang	Lalita Prasida Sripada Srisai	Anurudh Ganesan
Where are they from?	1 _____	5 _____	9 _____
What did they invent?	2 _____ _____	6 _____ _____	10 _____ _____
How old were they when they invented this?	3 _____	7 _____	11 _____
Why is their invention important?	4 _____ _____	8 _____ _____	12 _____ _____

2 Explain how each person's invention works.

1 Raymond Wang:

_____

2 Lalita Prasida Sripada Srisai:

_____

3 Anurudh Ganesan:

_____

Reading: research

SB pp.166–167

Research another teenage inventor. Find answers to the questions in the table in Activity 1 above and write a paragraph to add to the article.

_____

_____

_____

_____

_____

Vocabulary: useful verbs and nouns

SB p.168

Complete the sentences with the words from the box.

vaccines	filters	spreading	attaching	germs

1 Raymond's invention stops _____ from _____.

2 Lalita hopes that her invention, which _____ water, will be used in places where people don't have clean water.

3 Anurudh's invention is a way of _____ a bicycle to a plastic cooler, which means that _____ can be kept cool.

Use of English: relative clauses with prepositions

SB p.168

Read and match.

1 Raymond is the inventor
2 That's the building
3 The man with
4 The bicycle
5 The aeroplanes in
6 This invention,

a in which he made his invention.
b whom she is speaking invented this watch.
c to whom we gave the award.
d for which the inventor received no prizes, has changed the world.
e on which you are sitting could be used to transport medicines.
f which we travel can cause the spread of diseases.

Use of English: verb + –ing form or verb + to + verb

SB p.168

1 Write the words from the box under the correct heading in the table below.

imagine	consider	appear	continue	manage	prefer
	intend	avoid	offer		

followed by –ing form	followed by to + verb	followed by –ing form or to + verb
1 _____	4 _____	7 _____
2 _____	5 _____	8 _____
3 _____	6 _____	9 _____

2 Check that you know how to use the verbs in Activity 1. Write six sentences below using six of these verbs.

1 _____

2 _____

3 _____

4 _____

5 _____

6 _____

3 Complete the sentences with the correct form of the verb.

1 Will you consider _____ (stay) another day?

2 I didn't manage _____ (finish) my homework.

3 Do you prefer _____ (do) winter sports or summer sports?

4 He continued _____ (learn) the piano.

5 I always avoid _____ (eat) seafood.

6 He offered _____ (drive) me home.

Vocabulary: inventions

SB p.169

Complete the text with the words from the box.

> discovery   potential   transform
>
> significant   technology   ~~development~~

What do I think was the most important [1] _development_ in medicine in the twentieth century? [2] _____ has been very important with the invention of laser surgery and 3-D printing. But I would have to say that the most [3] _____ thing was the [4] _____ of antibiotics by Alexander Fleming in the 1920s. Doctors quickly realised the [5] _____ of this to [6] _____ medicine and save millions of lives.

Use of English: present perfect passive

SB p.170

1 Complete the sentences with the present perfect passive form of the verbs in brackets.

1 All the lights _have been switched off_ (switch off).
2 The money _____ (steal) from the safe.
3 A new species of bird _____ (discover).
4 This essay _____ (not / write) properly.
5 How many of these inventions _____ (sell)?
6 Sarah _____ (not / invite) to the party.

2 Correct the mistakes in these sentences. One is correct.

1 Has dinner being cooked yet?

_____

2 Two computers has been stolen from the school.

_____

3 John's phone has been damaging because he dropped it.

_____

4 A new type of medicine has been produce.

_____

5 The girl has been taken to hospital.

_____

6 Hundreds of books has been destroyed in the fire.

_____

Focus on Science

SB p.172

Read and circle the correct option.

1 What type of microbe causes the flu?

  a virus

  b bacteria

  c antibody

2 Which of these is *not* a way of spreading infectious diseases?

  a drinking infected water

  b breathing infected air

  c having a vaccine

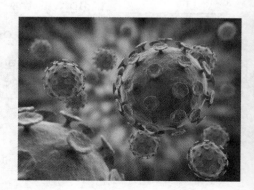

3 Which type of cell can kill or help to kill harmful microbes?

   a white blood cells

   b red blood cells

   c antibodies

4 What substances stick to microbes to make them easier to kill?

   a white blood cells

   b red blood cells

   c antibodies

5 When was a modern form of immunisation first used?

   a 1928

   b many centuries ago

   c 1796

Check your progress

My learning What did you learn in this unit?

1 What can you do now?

  I can …

   read an article about teenage inventors ☐

   use prepositions in relative clauses and the present perfect passive ☐

   write a story about an invention ☐

   understand infectious diseases ☐

   make and play a game about inventions ☐

2 Answer the questions about this unit.

  1 What have you enjoyed most?

  _____

  2 Is there anything you have found difficult?

  _____

  3 What would you like to learn more about?

  _____

Vocabulary: useful adjectives SB p.177

Replace the underlined sections of the text with adjectives from the box.

| efficient | creative | cost-effective | impossible | reliable | exact |

My robot is called Bob. It is helpful and <u>always does tasks very successfully without wasting time or energy</u> [1] *efficient*. In the morning, it makes my breakfast. I like exactly 200 ml of milk on my cereal. It never gets this wrong because it is <u>accurate</u> [2] _____ in everything it does. It does all my shopping for me, which is always <u>good because he gets a lot of things for the money</u> [3] _____. It is also <u>a good machine that never breaks down</u> [4] _____. The only thing that it can't do is draw! It isn't very <u>good at having new ideas</u> [5] _____, but it is very useful! I think it would be <u>not possible</u> [6] _____ to find another robot, which is as good as Bob!

Use of English: nouns + prepositions SB p.177

1 Complete the sentences with the correct preposition.

1 Do you have any interest <u>in</u> having a robot that can do jobs at home?

2 Have you ever read a story _____ a robot?

3 What are the advantages _____ hiring a robot instead of a human to do a job?

4 What are the disadvantages _____ hiring a robot instead of a human to do a job?

5 What would be your reaction _____ having a robot teach you English?

2 Answer the questions in Activity 1 in your notebooks.

Use of English: question tags SB p.177

Complete the sentences with the correct question tag.

1 Robots can't replace teachers, <u>can they</u>?

2 There aren't any machines in this room, _____?

3 Surgeons are cleverer than robots, _____?

4 Robots will be more powerful than us, _____?

5 We won't need human workers in the future, _____?

6 You don't agree with this, _____?

Reading: comprehension

Read and write *True, False* or *Doesn't say*.

1 Tim says that robots do a lot of work in his car factory. _____

2 Tim says that robots can drive his cars too. _____

3 Paula thinks that by the 2030s more than half of all jobs will be done by robots. _____

4 Mina thinks that robots will explore space in future. _____

5 Mina thinks that robots won't be expensive. _____

6 Evan thinks that we should be careful when it comes to making robots intelligent. _____

Reading: thinking about the text

Do you agree or disagree with these statements from the article? Explain your answers.

1 *In the future, I think that robots are going to be used to do more and more jobs.*

_____

_____

2 *I'm worried because robots are doing more and more of our jobs, so we are cutting down the number of jobs that are available for people to do.*

_____

_____

3 *Robots will do all the boring jobs that humans don't want to do. This is an exciting opportunity because we can spend our time doing more interesting jobs.*

_____

_____

4 *I believe that robots are going to be sent into space to explore.*

_____

_____

5 *There will come a point when robots will have more intelligence than humans. When that happens, there's a real risk that we will be controlled by robots.*

_____

_____

Robots and the future   83

Vocabulary: abstract nouns

SB p.179

Complete the crossword with abstract nouns.

Abstract nouns

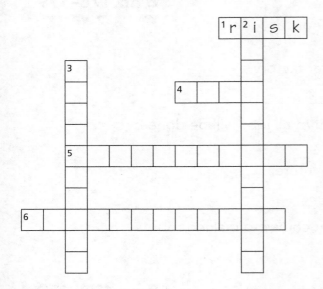

Across

1 a possibility that something bad will happen

4 what something or someone should do in a situation

5 a situation in which it is possible for you to do something that you want to do

6 when people want to work but can't because there aren't enough jobs for them

Down

2 a person is said to have this when they understand and learn things quickly and well

3 work you are paid for

Vocabulary: multi-word verbs with *cut*

SB p.180

Complete the sentences with *cut* + a preposition.

1 If we don't pay our bill then they might _____ our electricity.

2 Simon _____ the meat into little pieces for his dog.

3 My grandmother _____ the pieces of the dress and started to sew them together.

4 We must _____ on how much water we use by having showers instead of baths.

Use of English: future passive

SB p.180

1 Write the words in the correct order to make sentences.

1 space. / Robots / going to be / next month / are / sent into /

_____

2 done / By the 2030s, / a lot of / by robots. / be / will / our jobs

_____

3 won't / used / some countries. / be / in / These machines

_____

4 sold / This robot / isn't / to be / any more. / going

_____

5 driven / to be / Are we / going / by a robot car / tomorrow?

_____

6 found / on / Will / life / other planets? / be

_____

2 **Choose the correct options to complete the text.**

NEW ROBOTS ON SALE!

Next week, two brand new robots are going on sale! The first robot is

going to ¹ _____ called Tidybot and it's going to be

² _____ to do housework. The second robot is going to be

³ _____ as Chefbot and this one is going ⁴ _____ used

to cook food and prepare drinks too! Sit back and relax and let the

robots do your work for you!

Inventor of the robots, Julia Zane, said, "we're confident that people will

like the new robots and we think that many homes ⁵ _____ be

transformed by Tidybot and Chefbot!" Experts think that over 100 000

robots will be ⁶ _____ by the end of the year.

---

1 **a** being   **b** been   **c** be   **d** is
2 **a** use   **b** used   **c** using   **d** user
3 **a** know   **b** knew   **c** knowing   **d** known
4 **a** to   **b** be   **c** to be   **d** to being
5 **a** we'll   **b** will   **c** willing   **d** wheel
6 **a** sell   **b** sold   **c** selling   **d** sale

3 **Change the spelling in the sentences so that it is correct in British English.**
1 In the future, the world will be controled by robots. _____
2 This robot will never be equaled. _____
3 This road will be traveled by many students. _____
4 I think that tomorrow's meeting will be canceled. _____

1 **Look again at the text and answer the questions.**

1 How would you describe the character of Dr Frankenstein?

_____

2 What different settings are there in this extract?

_____

3 What different feelings does Dr Frankenstein have during this extract?

_____

4 How do you think the creature might feel?

_____

2 **Answer the questions.**

1 What things can you do to create excitement in a story?

_____

2 What did you enjoy about reading this extract of _Frankenstein_?

_____

3 Would you like to read the rest of the book? Why? Why not?

_____

Check your progress

1 What can you do now?

I can …

listen to a conversation about robot workers ☐

use nouns + prepositions, multi-word verbs with _cut_ and future passive ☐

read an article about the future of robots, discuss and write about the subject ☐

read an extract from Mary Shelley's _Frankenstein_ ☐

design a new robot ☐

2 Answer the questions about this unit.

1 What have you enjoyed most?

_____

2 Is there anything you have found difficult?

_____

3 What would you like to learn more about?

_____

My learning
What did you learn in this unit?

End-of-year review

Vocabulary: word hunt

Find four

jobs _____ _____ _____ _____

social media sites _____ _____ _____ _____

technological devices _____ _____ _____ _____

phrases you see in shop signs _____ _____ _____ _____

compound adjectives _____ _____ _____ _____

abstract nouns _____ _____ _____ _____

adverbs _____ _____ _____ _____

multi-word verbs _____ _____ _____ _____

Vocabulary: a crossword puzzle

Complete the crossword.

Across

3 when someone can't stop doing something that is bad for him / her

6 a place in a city where you can look at paintings or drawings

7 a person who writes a blog

8 a person that you don't know

Down

1 when people want to work but can't because there aren't enough jobs for them

2 a person who writes news stories

4 the person who has the idea for an invention

5 a plastic or cardboard box for food or drink

8 the money you get for doing a job

Writing: punctuation

Rewrite the sentences, adding in the missing punctuation and capital letters.

1 lets go and see a concert this weekend said sarah

_____

2 sorry i cant im doing a run to support a local charity replied danny

_____

3 thats great said sarah what charity are you supporting

_____

4 its a charity that helps disabled people do sports

_____

5 sarah said well done danny im proud of you

_____

Writing: spelling

Underline and correct the spelling mistake in each sentence. One sentence has no mistakes.

1 Sam is very confidant and generous. _____

2 This is possibly the best day of my life! _____

3 He opened his present immediatly. _____

4 He bought three loafs of bread because they were on special offer. _____

5 When I grow up I want to be an inventer. _____

6 We have traveled a long way to be here. _____

Writing: my year

Think about what you have learned this year in English and complete the sentences.

1 My favourite topic of the book was _____ because _____

_____.

2 I think that I am good at _____.

3 I think that I need more practice in _____.

4 This year in English, I am proud of myself because I have made progress with

_____.

5 Next year in English, I would like to learn how to _____.

Focus on grammar

1 Present and past continuous tenses [8Uf8]

a. The present continuous tense
   - is made with *am/is/are + -ing* form of the verb
   - is used to talk about actions that are continuing in the present
b. The past continuous tense
   - is made with *was/were + -ing* form of the verb
   - is used to talk about actions that were continuing in the present

See Section 5 for passive forms of these tenses.

2 Present perfect tense [8Uf3]

The present perfect tense
- is made with *have/has* (*not*) + past participle of the verb.
- links the past and the present. The action takes place in the past but there is always a connection with *now*.

The present perfect tense has three uses.

a. for something that *has happened recently*

   We sometimes use *just* when we talk about the recent past.

   The players have just arrived.
b. for something that started in the past and is still not finished

   We often use *for* and *since* when we talk about the unfinished past.
   - Use *since* with a point in time.

   Scientists have known about Komodo dragons since 1916.
   - Use *for* with a period of time.

   They have studied these strange creatures for over a hundred years.
c. for an experience

   We often use *ever* in questions and *never* in answers when we talk about experiences.

   Have you ever seen a Komodo dragon?

   No, I've never seen one in real life but I've seen them on television.

We often use time adverbs with the present perfect.
- yet = at any time up to now   *I haven't seen the new film **yet**.*
- just = a short time ago   *I've **just** seen the new film.*
- ever = at any time up to now   *Have you **ever** seen this film?*
- never = at no time up to now   *I've **never** seen the film.*

See Section 16 for more about adverbs.

3 Past perfect tense [8Uf7]

The past perfect tense
- is made with *had* (*not*) + past particple
- is used to talk about an earlier past (i.e. two steps into the past)

   By six o'clock yesterday, I had finished all my work.

- is often used with the past simple tense

  Before I went to Paris last month, I had flown in a plane only once.

4 Future forms

[8Uf4]

There are four ways to talk about the future in English:

	will arrive	
She	is going to arrive	
	is arriving	tomorrow evening at 19.00.
	arrives	

All of the sentences are correct. However, there are some differences in the use of each.

a. **will** + verb is used for
- sudden decisions (often with *I think*)

  I think I'll talk to my teacher tomorrow.   *I'm tired. I think I'll go to bed.*
- predicting or guessing

  In the future we will all go to university.   *I think it will rain tomorrow*
- future events you are certain about

  It will be my birthday next week.   *The teacher will be here in a minute.*

b. **be going to** + verb is used for
- something we have decided to do, or plans

  I'm going to fly to Lagos tomorrow.   *He's going to visit us on Friday.*
- future events we have evidence for

  Look at the sky! It's going to rain.   *Look at the time! We're going to be late.*

c. The **present continuous tense** is used for
- fixed or firm plans - often with a time, date or place

  I'm meeting him at six o'clock at the airport.   *They're arriving on Monday.*

d. The **present simple tense** is used for
- things which are timetabled to happen in the future

  His plane arrives at 08.30.   *What time does the exam begin tomorrow?*

See Section 5 for passive forms of these tenses.

5 Passive forms

[8Uf5]

- A passive can be used with any of the verb tenses: we use the verb *be* in the appropriate tense + past participle. Some examples:

PRESENT SIMPLE PASSIVE:	The *film*	is	chosen	by the manager.
PRESENT CONTINUOUS PASSIVE:	The book	is being	written.	
PAST SIMPLE PASSIVE:	The car	was	washed	by my sister.
PAST CONTINUOUS PASSIVE:	We	were being	followed.	
PRESENT PERFECT PASSIVE:	A dog	has been	found.	
FUTURE WITH *will*:	We	will be	followed.	
FUTURE WITH *going to*:	We	are going to be	followed.	

- We use passives when we don't know, we don't want to say or it is not important who did something. Passives are often used in reports.

  My money was stolen. (I don't know who took it.)

  A window has been broken. (I don't want to say that I broke it.)

  A lot of rice is eaten in Asia. (It is not important who eats it.)
- When we use a passive and want to say who did something, we use *by* ...

  A telephone call was made by my mother.

6 Modal verbs [8Uf10]

- Modal verbs add meaning to main verbs. They are not used about facts. They are used to express ability, possibility, certainty, requests, suggestions, necessity, etc.
- The modal verbs are *can, could, may, might, must, shall, should, will, would, ought to*. We also use *have to* and *need to* for the same purpose.
- Past modal verbs *should/shouldn't have* are used to express regret and criticism.
- We use modal verbs before main verbs and in short answers.

  You must hurry up.   Can you wait a minute?   No, I can't?
- Modal verbs only have one form (they do not add *-s, -ing* or *-ed*).
- After a modal we use the simple form of the main verb.

  You may go.   We should wait.
- Modal verbs do not need *do/does/did* in questions.

  Could you help me? (NOT ~~Do you could help me?~~)

7 if/unless/if only/wish that [8Uf11]

The unlikely conditional

- is used to talk about the result of things which are not likely to happen.

  If it snowed, I would be surprised.   I'd be very happy if I had my own plane.
- has two clauses.
  - The *If* clause has a verb in the simple past tense.
  - The main clause has *would* (or *wouldn't*) and a verb in the simple form.

    If it rained, we would be happy. They wouldn't believe me if I said that you were here.
- can replace *if + not* with *unless*.

  If it wasn't safe, I wouldn't take you. = Unless it was safe, I wouldn't take you.
- can be used to give advice.

  If I were you, I would see a doctor tomorrow.
- can be used to express a wish.

  If I had lots of money, I would buy my mother a car.

  If only/wish that
- are used with the past perfect to express regret and criticism.

  If only I had arrived on time.   If only I hadn't eaten all that cake.

  I wish I had arrived on time.   I wish I hadn't eaten all that cake.

- When we use reported speech the place, time and speaker has usually changed from the time and place that the words were spoken. For this reason we often have to change the verb tenses, pronouns and 'time and place' words.

- The tenses change like this:

tense change	speaking	reported speech
present simple ➔ past simple	"I **walk** to school."	He said he **walked** to school.
present continuous ➔ past continuous	"He **is working**."	She said he **was working**.
past simple ➔ past perfect	"I **played** football."	He said he **had played** football.
present perfect ➔ past perfect	"We **have missed** school every day."	I said we **had missed** school every day.

- Examples of how time and place words change:

now	➔	*then*
today	➔	*that day*
yesterday	➔	*the day before*
tomorrow	➔	*the next day*
next week/month/year	➔	*the following week/month/year*
last week/month/year	➔	*the week/month/year before*
here	➔	*there*

- When we report on a situation that has not changed (the time and place are still the same) then we do not have to change the verb tense. This happens when

   ○ we repeat something immediately after it is said:

   "He is arriving soon."   *"What did you say?"*   *"I said he is arriving soon."*

   ○ we are talking about something which is still true or always true:

   "My name is William."   *He said his name is William.*

   "Water boils at 100°C."   *The teacher told us that water boils at 100°C.*

- The most common verbs for reporting are *said* and *told*. There is an important difference in the way they are used.

   ○ We use *told* when we say **who** somebody is talking to.

   *Adu **told his wife** that there was a problem. I **told you** that I would help.*

   ○ We use *said* in other cases.

   ***Adu said** that there was a problem. **I said** that we would meet later.*

- To report a command, use *told* + noun/pronoun + *to* + verb.

   The teacher said, "Cal, sit down."

   The teacher told Cal to sit down.

- To report a request, use *asked* + noun/pronoun + *to* + verb.

   Jan said, "Help me carry this box, please."

   Jan asked me to help him carry a box.

- To report a *Wh-question*, use *asked* and the word order of a statement (not a question). Do not use a question mark.

He said, "Where are you going?"
The man asked where I was going.

- To report a *yes/no* question, use *asked + if*.
My mother said, "Are you feeling well?"
My mother asked if I was feeling well.

See Section 10 for polite questions inside statements or questions.

9 Relative clauses [8Ut11, 8Ut6]

- Relative clauses are used to give information about a noun. They allow us to make sentences longer and more interesting.
- There are two types of relative clauses:

a. A **defining relative clause** tells us who or what the noun is. It is an important part of a sentence. If we take it out we might not know what the noun is we are talking about.
*The doctor **who you saw yesterday** is away today.*

b. A **non-defining relative clause** gives us extra information about the noun. We can take it out of the sentence and still understand it. We use commas to separate it from the rest of the sentence.
*The doctor, **who is now over 70**, is resting.*

- The first word of a relative clause is usually a relative pronoun.
  - **who** – refers to a person
    - *I saw a man **who** has a wooden leg.*
  - **which** – refers to an animal or a thing
    - *There is the dog **which** bit me.*
  - **that** – can replace *who* and *which* to refer to a person, animal or thing
    - *I saw a man **that** has a wooden leg. There is the dog **that** bit me*
- Relative pronouns replace other pronouns in the relative clause – don't use both.
My mother has a friend who ~~she~~ is a singer.
- We can use *why* in a relative clause to give reasons.
*The reason **why** I like her is that she always has time to help.*
- We can use *where* in a relative clause to talk about a place.
*This is the place **where** I live.*
- We can use *when* in a relative clause to talk about a time.
*2015 was the year **when** my brother was born.*
- We can use *whose* in a relative clause to talk about possession.
*This is the boy **whose** coat I borrowed.*
- We can use prepositions in relative clauses. In formal English, they go before the relative pronoun and in informal English, they go at the end of the sentence.
*New York is the city **from** where my friend comes.*
*New York is the city where my friend comes **from**.*

*Ben Marsh is the man **to** whom the prize was given.*
*Ben Marsh is the man who the prize was given **to**.*

10 Question forms

[8Ut5]

- We can use prepositions in questions, too. In formal English, they go before the question word and in informal English, they go at the end of the sentence.

  At *what time did the lesson start?*   *What time did the lesson start* **at**?

  In *which direction did Mel go?*   *Which direction did Mel go* **in**?

  From *whose class is this student?*   *Whose class is this student* **from**?

- When we want to ask a question politely, we can put it inside another question or statement.

  Direct question: *What time did he arrive?*

  Indirect questions: **Could you tell me** *what time he arrived?*

  I wonder *if you could tell me what time he arrived.*

  Do you know *what time he arrived?*

11 *to* + verb after adjectives and verbs

[8Ut8]

- After adjectives, we use *to* + verb.

  I'm shocked to hear the news.   *We're likely to stay for dinner. He's certain to arrive on time.*

- After some verbs, we use *to* + verb.

  I promise to help you.   *He appears to be happy.*

12 *-ing* forms after prepositions and verbs

[8Ut9]

- After a preposition, we use the *-ing* form of a verb.

  I dream about becoming a vet.   *Are you interested in studying French?*

- After some verbs, we use the *-ing* form of a verb.

  He suggested talking to you.   *He avoided sitting in the sun.*

13 Pronouns

[8Ut6, 8Ut7]

- Pronouns take the place of nouns, e.g. *she, it, them, ours.*
- We use **indefinite pronouns** when we don't know, or don't want to say, exactly who or what we are talking about:

everybody	everyone	everything
somebody	someone	something
anybody	anyone	anything
nobody	no one	nothing

- We use **demonstrative pronouns** when we want to indicate what we're talking about by pointing at something.

  This *is beautiful.*   **That** *is my son.*   **These** *are my choices.*   **Those** *are my shoes.*

  These pronouns can also be used to refer to something that has just been mentioned in a sentence.

  I don't feel very well.   **This** *is why I don't want to go out.*

  He gave me chocolates and flowers.   **These** *were my birthday presents.*

- We use **reflexive pronouns** when we want to refer back to the subject of the sentence.

  *I gave **myself** time to relax.   Did you teach **yourself** English?   He cut **himself** with the knife.*

  *She helped **herself** to some cake.   The cat is washing **itself**.   We blamed **ourselves** for the mistake.*

  *Please help **yourselves** to whatever you need.   They looked after **themselves** all day.*
- See Section 9 for **relative pronouns** and Section 14 for **quantitative pronouns**.

14 Quantifiers [8Uf1, 8Ut4, 8Ut6]

- Quantifiers are small words that tell us about quantity, e.g. *some, many, a few*.
- Some quantifiers can be used only with countable nouns and some only with uncountable nouns. Others can be used with both.

	Countable		Uncountable		
	How many eggs do we have?		*How much money do we have?*		
We have	a large number of a lot of/lots of plenty of many some a few/several not many	eggs.	We have	a large amount of a lot of/lots of plenty of much some a little not much	money.

- We can use words like *all of, half of, twice*, etc. to tell us more information about the amount of something.

  We have been waiting all this time.   Half of my money was stolen.

15 Comparing [8Uf2, 8Ug4]

- When we compare with adjectives we can make the comparison stronger or weaker by using structures like *not as* + adjective + *as, just as* + adjective + *as, much* + comparative adjective + *than, slightly* + comparative adjective + *than*.

  I'm not as tall as you.   He's just as tall as you.

  He's much stronger than he was.   He's slightly stronger than he was.
- When we compare with adverbs we can make the comparison stronger or weaker by using structures like *not as* + adverb + *as, just as* + adverb + *as, far less/more* + adverb, *much* + comparative adverb + *than, slightly* + comparative adverb + *than*.

  This computer doesn't work as quickly as it used to.   Sarah runs just as quickly as Max.

  You drive far more carefully than your father.   It rained much more heavily than last week.

  The children sang slightly louder than they did before.
- We use *like* or *as* to say one thing is the same as another. They are called similes.
  - verb + *like* + noun phrase: *She's like a second mother to me. It disappeared like ice in the sun.*
  - *as* + adjective + *as*: *It was as cold as ice.   He ran as fast as a cheetah.*

16 Adverbs in different positions

[8Ug5, 8Ug6]

- Adverbs give information about *how*, *where*, *when* or *how often* an action happens, or *how certain* we are that it will happen.

  *You **always** laugh.   He is **certainly** waiting for us.   I can **never** eat this.*

- Adverbs that tell us *how*, *where* and *when* usually go at the end of a sentence. There can be more than one adverb in a sentence. The order for these adverbs is *how – where – when*.

  *They played **well in the match yesterday**.*

- Adverbs that tell us *when* can also go at the beginning of a sentence. We use a comma after the adverb. This gives the adverb more importance.

  I will help you when you arrive.   When you arrive, I will help you.

- Adverbs that tell us *how often* or *how certain* go before a main verb, and after a modal or *is/are/was/were/do/does/did*.

- Some adverbs describe the whole sentence rather than a particular verb and these come at the end of a sentence.

  *I loved this book, so I would like to read the sequel **as well**.* (to add information)

  *I loved this book, but I didn't like the sequel **though**.* (to add contrasting information)

17 Conjunctions

[8Ut10]

- Conjunctions connect two ideas in a sentence.
  - Some always go between the two ideas, e.g. *and*, *or*, *but*, *so*.
  - Others can go between the two ideas or at the beginning of the sentence. If the conjunction is at the beginning of the sentence, use a comma between the two ideas.

Although I like flying, I didn't enjoy that journey

- We use *so that* and *(in order) to* to explain a purpose.
  - *I studied hard **so that** I would do well in my exam.*
  - *We opened the window **(in order) to** let some air in.*
- We use *although* and *though* to contrast two ideas:
  - ***Although** I don't have a lot of free time, I always make time to read in the evenings.*
  - *I don't usually like non-fiction, **though** I love reading autobiographies.*
- We use *while* and *whereas* to balance two contrasting ideas.
  - ***While** I don't enjoy comedy, my sister loves it.*
  - *I always read quickly, **whereas** my friend reads slowly.*